Roger Burke
Psalm 19:14

Miracle in a Hay Field

a collection of short stories

ROGER BURKE

iUniverse, Inc.
Bloomington

Miracle in a Hay Field
a collection of short stories

Copyright © 2010 Roger Burke

iUniverse books may be ordered through booksellers or by contacting:

iUniverse
1663 Liberty Drive
Bloomington, IN 47403
www.iuniverse.com
1-800-Authors (1-800-288-4677)

ISBN: 978-1-4502-7436-4 (pbk)
ISBN: 978-1-4502-7437-1 (ebk)

Printed in the United States of America

iUniverse rev. date: 11/18/2010

INTRODUCTION

Most of these stories were written weekly from July 11, 2004 until May 28th 2006 from personal experience for the First Baptist Church bulletin, Polk, Nebraska. The purpose for the stories was a kind of entrée for the message of that day.

Other stories were written while I endured the pain of a pinched sciatic nerve as I waited from January 1 until February 11, 2010 for spine surgery.

It is my sincere desire and prayer that the Lord Jesus will be honored through the stories and that you will find them a delightful and challenging resource for your inspiration and perhaps even a good laugh.

Read and enjoy!
Roger Burke

The Partners (1+1=1)
Roger and Wilma Burke

SPECIAL RECOGNITION

I offer my heart felt tribute to my parents, Verdy and Geneva Burke, and grandparents, Joseph and Gladys Gruver, and George and Ellen Burke, who provided the material I needed to meet the one who is the foundation of life itself.

I am grateful for Wilma, my loving and generous wife of 61 years, and the fruit of her womb: Marjorie, Doris, Timothy, Roxane, and Philip; plus the addition of 24 grandchildren and 29 (and adding) great grandchildren. I am especially grateful for the encouragement and help given by daughter Doris, the pictorial editor and grand daughter Brittany, & her husband Bobby, the editors in chief for this enterprise.

Finally, I salute my Savior, in the words of a Gospel song, "How rich I am since Jesus came my way redeemed my soul and turned my night to day, how rich, how very rich I am."

Roger A Burke

CONTENTS

Mom and dad's wedding party. October 25, 1925
(Evelyn Burke, Geneva Burke, Verdy Burke, Clifford Gruver)

1. THE RUN-A-WAY

My Dad and Mom were married on the 23rd of October 1925 and began as they called it back then, "keeping house." Actually, they rented the Larson place about 2 miles west of Grandpa and Grandma Burke's. They had a few cows and young stock, probably eight in total and Dad bought a perfectly matched team of dapple grey mares, named Polly and Katie (right off the prairie, unbroken and drugged).

The horses began acting a bit strange about the third day, throwing their heads, etc. That evening, Dad decided to hook them to the bobsled and visit his folks. Mom and the dog were sitting on the sled as they drove to the end of the drive way where Dad got off to open the gate. No one knows what or why, but the horses turned away from the gate and at full speed headed across a small meadow. Mom fell off the sled in 50 feet or so, the dog stayed on until the plank box flipped off the bunks.

The horses ran into a fence about 300 feet from the gate, one went down, and both were tangled in the wire. Dad cut all the wires but one and gave the cutter to Mom. He stood between the horses holding on to the bridles and said, "Cut the last wire." When she snipped the wire the horses reared up and headed north with Dad suspended between them. He tried to climb on top of the neck yoke but it was bobbing up and down too crazily for him to make it. He tried to swing to the side, but the horses front legs batted him down. He knew they would straddle a stump or a tree and run the sled tongue through him. He thought, my only chance is to drop in the snow and hope I can go under the sled.

He dropped, but a pin through the bolster clipped his head. It was dark enough so that Mom couldn't see him. She kept calling his name but he didn't answer until she was nearly hysterical, finally he said, "Go to the house and heat some water." Then she knew he was hurt, but could only imagine how much. The horses traveled about a hundred feet after Dad dropped before they stumbled and ran the sled tongue into the ground. Dad caught up with them and managed to get them loose from the sled and the neck yoke off of one before they took off into the night.

The next morning, when Dad opened the door of the house, the horses again headed away from him, out into the road, headed toward Grandpa's. The nearest neighbor, Gus Brengelson, had a telephone and saw the horses running with the harnesses dragging and the neck yoke flopping. He called Grandpa and said, "Verdy's horses are coming your way, and they look like they're running away." Grandpa headed them into a pasture where they were able to catch them.

No one was ever able to break Katie and she was finally sold to a Fox Farm for fox food. We kept Polly and bought a Bay mare, named Dolly. They were an excellent and stable team. Dolly got Sleeping sickness when she was 32 years of age and died. Polly now 28, fell apart when Dolly died. She roamed the fences hour after hour, day after day, nickering for her partner. Finally the end was so obvious that Dad gave in and called the Fox farm; "Take her, but don't let me know when" He told them. We were milking one morning when we heard the shot. We didn't say a word but I saw the tears running down Dad's cheeks and if anyone had looked my cheeks were wet too.

Revelation 6:2 I looked, and behold, a white horse, and he who sat on it had a bow; and a crown was given to Him, and he went out conquering and to conquer.

2. ANXIETY

Our family was having a discussion about memory. I said, "I remembered going with Mom to a garage sale at a Mrs. Keene's home". Mom said, "I don't think so. You weren't two years old (1928)."

So to preserve my integrity I began describing in detail what I remembered. I remembered that the house was near the edge of town with a railroad track right next to it. I said, "When we went inside it was a narrow room with an archway or big double doors with lots of stuff leaning against the walls." Mom stopped me and said, "You remember it better than I do."

The depression hit us in 1929, Dad had just bought the farm and times were tough. Yet, in spite of my good memory I do not remember my parents ever making me feel anxious about our situation. I know they talked to each other about land payments and groceries, shoes, overalls, coats and feed for the chickens pigs and cows. But I never felt like we might lose our home or may not have anything to eat or wear.

I remember my Dad telling some of the neighbors when the worst of the depression was over (about 1938), how he and Mom had prayed and every time a payment was due, or an unexpected bill came, God faithfully supplied the need. I remember the tender loving way he praised God, giving the Lord full credit for the ability to clear the debt on the farm ahead of schedule.

Dad and Mom's tender loving care gave us good memories, teaching us not to be anxious about the things we couldn't control and to trust the Lord implicitly for everything else.

Philippians 4:6 Be anxious for nothing, but in everything by prayer and supplication with thanksgiving let your requests be made known to God.

The Larson Place – My first home
(Prunes, who was a friendly mut that was also
part timber wolf, in the window box)

Roger and Prunes on the family farm
(Purchased in 1928, brother Ken and sister Verly would be
born here. Grandpa Burke's farm is in the background)

3. THE HOUSE ON THE FARM

How do you get from point A to point B when there are no marked streets or avenues? That's the way it was when I came into this world, August 1, 1926. The answer is by personal names and landmarks. I still remember some of those names, Luloffs, Burke's, Berggren's, Meyer's, Knife Lake, Ann River, Alcohol Creek, etc.

I was born on the Larsen farm about nine miles north-west of Mora, Minnesota, next door to the Hornes. The house, 24' X 26', divided ½ living room, the other ½ divided between kitchen and bedroom. It was a shack by today's standards, but it was my first home. It had a path to the "little house" and no indoor plumbing. I lived in that house again in 1948. It was still the same shack. The gravel pit was still in the front yard, the toilet facilities were still in the house of many names (back house, biffy, outhouse, privy, two holer). The field mice had their own private entrance through a hole in the kitchen floor.

We moved from the Larsen place in 1927 to the Berg place just across the road from Grandpa and Grandma Burke. The Berg house, similar to the Larson shack, was a temporary home for us as we waited to move to the farm Dad had purchased. Years later, 1936, give or take a few years, Dad purchased the Berg place. It was the house where Uncle Dick died. It would become a club house for my brother and I and some of our cousins. We pretty much ended its history.

Sometime in 1928 we moved to the farm where I would spend the next 17 years and where my brother Ken and sisters, Elaine and Verly would be born. The farm buildings included a bungalow style barn, a chicken house, a granary and a house. The house was a two story, hip roof structure about 24' by 26' with a screened in porch on the west end and an enclosed entry across two thirds of the south side. The main house was kitchen, dining room, and front room with an area about 8' by 12' for a hallway, and pantry and a stairway that led to the three bedrooms upstairs. The lower level was a log structure, covered with beaver board and siding when the upstairs and porches were added. The logs and beaver board made a perfect home for bed bugs. We finally had to fumigate (cyanide, I think), and that solved the problem. We still had the path instead of a bath and until I was nearly through High School, the running water was available if you ran to fetch it.

We added to the buildings a bigger chicken house, which we eventually moved and attached to the barn for a calf nursery and housing for the pigs. We also built a milk house/garage combo where we installed a 32 volt Delco generator for electricity. This is also where we positioned our DeLaval cream separator and coolers for the milk as well as our shop tools

My parents and my brother have all gone home to be with the Lord, but my sisters and I still remember nostalgically those days back home on the farm.

Joshua 24:15b But as for me and my house, we will serve the Lord.

The original barn and two-year-old Roger
(The barn was expanded to house about 35 head of stock)

4. GROWING UP POOR

The parsonage for my first Pastoral ministry was the house in which I was born. It gained its notoriety from the amenities it didn't have: no indoor plumbing, no running water, no electricity, no basement and mice entering and exiting at their leisure.

We moved from that place in 1927 to another shack before finally purchasing a farm in 1928. Then in 1929 the banks crashed. Money was as scarce as the proverbial "hens teeth". Poverty was real. My mother's folks had homesteaded 80 acres on property owned by the Ann River Logging Company and purchased another 80 acres for $10 an acre. They lost it all in the depression of the 1930's.

Was it discouraging? Sure, but we held our chins up and kept on going. We had each other, neighbors helped neighbors. We had our church family so we worshipped, prayed, visited, shared the work, pulled together, drank coffee, and with sweat, toil, and tears ate the fruit of the land. We were survivors!

Those were good times we had together back then. Today it's called "Quality time". We were innovative problem solvers, sharing our meager fare, encouraging each other, laughing together and enjoying the trip.

Poverty didn't make us criminal or produce juvenile delinquents to the contrary it made us strong. It developed community!

I am personally blest by every memory of those hard but delightful experiences of growing up poor with family and friends who loved me. I can relate to the be-attitudes: *remember*.

Matthew 5:3 "Blessed are the poor in spirit, for theirs is the kingdom of heaven.

Roger and Kenny outside the house that didn't burn

5. FIRE

When day light faded at our farm, there were hogs to slop, chickens to feed and cows to milk.

Arriving home late one Sunday evening, the summer of 1930, Dad, with a severe headache, took a couple of aspirin and lay down on the couch while Mom changed clothes and headed to the barn.

Dad didn't plan on a nap so when he woke up, realizing Mom had gone to do chores, he quickly changed his clothes and headed for the barn leaving my brother, Ken (age 1 1/2) and I (age 4) alone in a rapidly darkening house.

I had seen the folks light the Coleman lantern that hung over the dinning room table many times and figured I can do that. I got a match, pushed a step stool up to the table, climbed on to the table, pumped air into the gas tank, turned on the valve, struck the match, and it went out. Without turning the valve off (my big mistake) I went to get another match. When I struck the second match, everything on the table, dad's suit coat, the Sunday paper, and the table cloth, was on fire.

I tried to put it out but realized I couldn't stop the fire so I put Ken on his kitty-car, pushed him out into the middle of the yard, and ran to the barn yelling, FIRE!

Mom and Dad were able to put the fire out and my hair grew back. I was sure I would be punished, but instead I was praised for doing the right thing with my brother and by alerting Mom and Dad.

Kurt Kaiser in his song, *Pass it On,* wrote, *"It only takes a spark to get a fire going".* With so much of our world in spiritual darkness, some one ought to strike a match!

Jesus said:

Matthew 5:14 "You are the light of the world".

6. LAZY DICK

Evelyn, one of my Dad's sisters married a man, old enough to be her dad, by the name of Richard. Dick was the only name I ever knew him by, except that many of his brothers and sisters-in-law and some of the neighbors prefaced it with the word "Lazy" because he was always looking for a place to lie down.

Early summer in 1935 my Aunt Evelyn accompanied Dick to the Doctor's office and asked the Doctor why Dick was always tired. The Doctor was surprised and responded, "You mean your husband hasn't told you that he's full of cancer and has but a few months at the most to live?"

That was the end of the nick name "Lazy" and some very embarrassed folks began trying to find forgiveness for their terrible misjudgment.

Uncle Dick died a very painful death that December in 1935. There was little pain medication back then and few went to the hospital. I remember them trying to pour a liquid broth into him through a tube and the liquid exiting through a tube in his side as cancer had destroyed so much of his insides.

Most of all, though I was only 9 years old, I remember his death. Uncle Dick had been comatose for a time. His breathing was labored and shallow when suddenly he opened his eyes, turned toward his wife and asked, "Am I in heaven?" "No," she replied, "you're still here with me." "But," he closed his eyes as he said, "I hear such beautiful music. Oh, Oh yes! They are coming for me!" His body lay still. The agony of pain was replaced by a sweet restful peace. Lazy Dick was dead! But we all knew that Richard was with Jesus.

2 Corinthians 5:8 We are of good courage, I say, and prefer rather to be absent from the body and to be at home with the Lord.

7. COMMUNITY

If you drew a circle big enough to encompass District 24, "Lowell," a one room rural school, where I attended eight years as had my Dad and all his brothers and sisters before me, the circle would have a diameter of about two and a half miles and encompass 30-35 farms.

Our neighbors were for the most part good people. They were Baptists, Lutherans, and Catholics, with a few who didn't attend any church. There were Swedes, Norwegians, Germans, and French, divided politically between the Democratic-Farmer Labor and Republican parties. Few were blood relatives except for my grandparents and uncles and aunts still living at home.

Some of us visited back and forth and we all pitched in when it came time for threshing or sawing wood or removing snow from the roads.

There were differences too. All were poor, but some were cheap poor, some were generous poor, some were lazy poor, and some were sloppy poor. There were few who were skilled but everyone had an opinion. Morally and ethically we were all pretty much on the same page but spiritually there was a noticeable difference.

Life back then, as it has always been, was the challenge of getting along with one's neighbors. Jesus framed it this way, "Love your neighbor as you love yourself." So it isn't just getting along as many try to do, but in making a positive loving impression on each other for Jesus sake.

The Apostle Paul quoted the rule again:

Galatians 5:14 For the whole Law is fulfilled in one word, in the statement, "You shall love your neighbor as yourself."

8. PRESSURE POINT

One of my summer jobs before I was a teenager was to lead our Holstein bull to water by a chain fastened to a ring in his nose. I doubt I weighed 70 pounds; the bull was all of 1800 pounds. If the bull would have objected he could have, except for the pressure on the ring in his tender nose, changed his mind. One might say my wish was his command.

In Isaiah 36-37 God speaks to Hezekiah concerning the Assyrian invasion under King Sennacherib. Isaiah delivered God's message sent specifically to Hezekiah. "Don't be afraid," God said, "for I will put My hook in Sennacherib's nose and My bridle in his lips and turn him back by the way which he came."

Solomon lusted after many women, they turned his heart away after other gods and splintered the kingdom he left his son.

It doesn't take a lot of pressure, if plied in the right place, to take a wicked person and propel them to judgment, or to take a righteous person and turn them to wickedness.

If a Holstein bull, or a powerful king like Sennacherib, can be led by the nose, and if a wise king like Solomon can be defeated by lust, who am I to think I can handle life all by myself?

Therefore I will set my mind on things above not on things of this earth so that the pressure points are directed by the Lord Jesus.

Hebrews 12:2 ^(NASB) *Fixing our eyes on Jesus, the author and perfecter of faith, who for the joy set before Him endured the cross, despising the shame, and has sat down at the right hand of the throne of God.*

Lowell School District 24
Lowell School closed in the spring of 1954,
ending 56 years of education.
Grandpa George Burke built the school. My dad, all of his siblings,
as well as myself and all of my siblings attended this school.

9. JESUS – SANTA

Lowell, district 24, grades 1-8, always had a Christmas Program. Long before White Christmas was written in 1942, they were standard in central Minnesota. I doubt any of us knew what chestnuts were and few, if any, had a fireplace to roast them in anyway. The school program traditionally featured little poetic pieces, a short skit or two, a few songs, and Santa Claus. Santa, in my memory, had center stage. Jesus' birth, in hind sight, appears to have been more patronized than celebrated. I remember quite vividly the stomping feet of a neighbor dressed up like Santa, with a large bag of presents for all the children and a big gift for the teacher. The climax was the traditional gift for Alfred Peterson. Alfred was an old bachelor age 45, (give or take a year) who lived just north of the school, walked with his hands behind his back and talked to himself, which we all thought was a little odd.

Most of us believed that Christmas was for celebrating the birth of Jesus, but school wasn't church. There was no attempt by anyone to negate or denigrate the birth of Jesus. We just enjoyed the freedom of a hearty "Ho-ho" and the mythical Jolly Old Saint Nicholas! My family was one of a very few who had a radio, but nonetheless, everyone was aware of the message "Santa Clause is coming to Town", sung by Eddie Cantor in 1934. And although most of us believed that Santa was a mythical figure, we thought, why take a chance.

I scolded the young people in our youth group one time for frivolous behavior during our devotions. They needed to realize that maturity is learning to live free responsibly. When we put on Christ, we don't discard our joy, our fun, our hilarity. When we put on Christ, we put on the fullness of Joy! I pity the saint who takes his religion so seriously that he's afraid to let his hair down with a hearty, Ho, Ho, Ho!

When it comes to Christmas, there is no contest between Christ and Santa Claus. Over 700 years before Jesus was born, Isaiah penned the words, "Behold a virgin will be with child and bear a son and she will call His name Immanuel."And in the fullness of time that came to pass in a Bethlehem stable. Our faith is grounded in history! Santa on the other hand offers only a short trip to temporarily get out of Kansas and enjoy the make-believe Land of Oz.

Christian maturity is in knowing what passes away and what endures; knowing how to balance temporal imagination with eternal truth. Christmas is for celebrating with great joy and awe, the greatest gift ever given and Santa doesn't offer anything even close to that. But don't throw the baby out with the bath water, a few jollies appropriately administered can free us up without hindering our worship, and a meaningful encounter with the God who so loved that He gave His Son.

Psalm 126:2 (the Lord had restored the fortunes of Zion) "***Then our mouth was filled with laughter and our tongue with shouts of joy.***"

10. BOILS

I was 11 with a big problem, every time I put my foot down the boil on the side of my ankle throbbed with excruciating pain. Those ugly pimples caused an infection, common back in the 30's.

My Dad at 18 had several boils on his right arm. They were beginning to heal so he volunteered to take lunch to the men working in the field. Riding his 1916 Harley Motorcycle he lost control and went into the ditch, slid on his right side and scraped all the boils off his arm. Needless to say he had pain big time!

Boils had a core at the center which either had to erupt or be lanced before healing could begin.

We had a hired man in 1936 (we called Jim Whoody) with a boil under his chin. The Doctor told him it needed to be lanced but Jim put it off. Well we were in the barn one day and Jim was being mean to me so I said, "If you don't quit I'll hit you on your boil." Jim stuck his chin out and replied, "You wouldn't dare." So I nailed him! Then I headed for the house screaming for my Mom, who promptly came to my rescue.

Boils are bad news but fade into insignificance when measured against leprosy.

Leprosy in the Bible is a type of sin. Sin is a disease of the soul, mind, and body. It is a stench in the nostrils of God and its prognosis is death. But, in mercy and grace, God sent His Son to the cross in our place, paying our penalty offering us divine life as a free gift instead of death.

There came a day when I knelt at the altar, pled for forgiveness, surrendered my old life and received in Jesus a living and eternal hope.

John 1:12 — as many as received Him, to them He gave the right to become children of God, even to those who believe in His name.

11. THE REALITY OF DEATH

Life gets real serious when it hangs in the balance while death waits in the shadows. Death is not a welcome guest at our parties, and most of us will, as Gloria Gaither said, "Tie one more knot in the end of the rope" to keep it at bay as long as possible. Hope becomes a valuable resource for all who sense the approach of the grim reaper.

I have been with the dying hundreds of time and hundreds of times with the families of the deceased, and confess that what happens between life and death is a mystery; one moment the dying may be smiling, joking, the next, unresponsive and dead. Those who have received life in Jesus will sorrow, but their sorrow is overpowered by hope. My cousin Marjorie said of her imminent death from cancer, "I'm not afraid of what's beyond death for I know I will be with Jesus, but I have never died before and I'm concerned about dying."

Melvin, three years of age, the youngest member of the Tom Johnson family, always stood by the fence surrounding the Johnson's front yard as we drove our cattle to pasture. His dog "Tag" was always with him and Melvin would say, "Sick 'em Tag." I was glad Tag never obeyed Melvin's command. A Scarlet Fever epidemic swept through our neighborhood and I was told that Melvin had caught the disease. I was eleven, or nearly so, and had no idea of the danger Scarlet Fever posed.

So that morning in 1937, as I came into the kitchen looking for breakfast, Mom said, "Melvin died last night." That was my first introduction to death. I remember wondering what that was like. Was Melvin really gone? Where did he go? Will I ever see him again? I even wondered if Tag knew his buddy was gone.

My mom told me that though we would miss him a lot, he was safe with Jesus in heaven. She said, "Jesus really loves children and must have thought Melvin was special to call him home so early."

Later I learned that the Scarlet Fever had caused an abscess in Melvin's throat and though Melvin was over the Scarlet Fever, the abscess had broken and Melvin had bled to death while his parents, in total helplessness, watched him die.

I learned three things during those days.

1. Parents will do anything to help their children live.
2. Parents appreciate, beyond words, those who care enough to help them cope.
3. Parents, indeed all of us in the icy grip of death, long with all our hearts for a ray of hope.

The hope we all need is not like someone saying, "Boy, I sure hope he got the message." No it's hope defined in **Hebrews 11:1,** "Faith is the assurance of things hoped for, the conviction of things not seen." It's Peter's conviction **I Peter 1:3-** "A living hope through the resurrection of Jesus Christ from the dead".

Romans 5:5 Hope does not disappoint, because the love of God has been poured out within our hearts through the Holy Spirit who was given to us.

12. THE BIKE ITCH

When you're eleven going on twelve and have never had a bike, the itch is unbearable. I've heard it said, "I want it so bad I can taste it." That was my itch for a bike. It occupied my thoughts day and night.

Then one day Dad and Mom took me with them to the Gambles Hardware store in our home town, Mora, Minnesota, to look at a used bike. The bike had a tag marked $5 on it. Dad said to the store owner, (I think his name was Harris), "I'll give you $2.50 now and $2.50 next week when I bring the cream to town. It sounded like a wonderful idea to me, but the owner said, "It has to be cash today."

I was not just angry, I was livid! I could not understand anyone doubting Dad's honesty. Think of it, he refused a 50% down payment and waiting just seven days for the total payment. The man obviously saw how much I wanted the bike but he just didn't care. What I saw was a mean spirited, compassionless jerk. I bawled and squalled all the way home. I held a grudge and boycotted the Gambles Store for five years. I'm sure he missed me...???

A few months went by and dad took our 1931 REO Speed Wagon 1 ½ ton truck and made the usual trip to Willmar, Minnesota for a load of corn for our feeder pigs. It was getting dark when he pulled into the yard and came in the house with a big smile on his face. I remember what he said as if it were yesterday, "Boys why don't you check the load?" My brother Ken and I raced to the truck. I, being older, got there first, shinnied up the side of the truck and there, laying on top of the load of corn, was a brand new Hiawatha, genuine Montgomery Wards, black with white trim, balloon-tired bicycle!

My desire for that old beat-up used bike was snuffed out. We had a new one! I discovered waiting paid better dividends than bawling and creating a fuss for somebody's old bike.

I think there's an analogy here for all Christians. We often want something so bad that we turned our covetous natures loose and bombarded God with our druthers, only to discover down the road a piece, that He had something much better waiting for us. All we needed was a little patience and a big helping of trusting the generosity of the Lord. He knows what we need.

Psalm 106:15 "He gave them their request, but sent leanness into their soul".

13. OUR NEIGHBORS

The mid-1930's were very dry, men actually cut trees so cattle could eat the leaves. One family lost half of their dairy herd trying to supplement their inadequate hay supply with willow brush. Dad bought 80 acres with another 40 fenced for pasture. The north end of the acreage had a 20 acre field, and across the road a quarter of a mile to the west lived our friends the Micks. The Mick family consisted of three boys (Bill, Taylor, John) and two girls (Nora and Essie), never married brothers and sisters. They were a bit isolated, surrounded on three sides by trees and swamps and a mile of low maintenance road from the nearest home. Their home was quite primitive, with limited electricity, a hand pump in the kitchen, cement floors, an old cook stove for preparing meals, and a potbellied stove in the living room for heat.

Bill was a big man, often referred to as the gentle giant. He was a soft spoken deacon in our Church. He loved the Lord Jesus with all his heart, and walked his talk. That was true of his brother Taylor and sisters, Nora and Essie. John was, to say the least, different. John never went to church, seldom stayed for the Bible Studies held in their home. He said if you kept the back of your neck warm in the winter you would never get a cold, so he sewed canvas on the ear-flaps of his cap. John also made pants out of white canvas in the fall, as the legs frayed at the ends he simply trimmed them; by the next summer he had shorts. Men often cut brush in their pastures and along the road and piled the brush they had cut. John either had a tendency toward pyromania, or just couldn't stand to see the brush piles, whatever the reason the brush piles always burned. We were concerned because no one watched the fire putting the whole area in danger.

I remember one dark night as we were going home from church a man stepped out in front of Bill's car and was killed. Bill was crushed, feeling that somehow he was at fault. We later learned the man intended to commit suicide and Bill just happened to be the first car that came along. One spring when the roads were terrible, my classmate from first grade through high school, George LaDouceur, got his car stuck. Taylor came by and offered to try to pull him out of the mud. The chain was fastened and Taylor took off, when he reached the end of the chain it snapped and one end of it went through George's windshield. Taylor meant well, but lacked towing experience.

We harvested the hay across from Mick's in August; it wasn't the best quality so it came last. We were busy pitching hay when we noticed several cars drive toward Mick's. When we saw the Doctor's car, we knew something had gone wrong. Then we saw John coming across the field. John sauntered up to us and said, "Well, Bill's dead." We were shocked, not just because Bill had died, but the cavalier way in which his brother reported it. "Bill's dead?" I queried, "How did it happen?" "Well," John said, "We were going to saw some wood and Bill started to crank the motor - he just fell there in the sawdust. He's too big to lift so we had to let him lay there. Now if it would have been me, I'm like Napoleon, I wouldn't weigh 95 pounds if I was soaking wet." That was John.

The Micks were good neighbors and even though they probably were among the poorest financially, they never hesitated to share what they had with anyone that came by.

Romans 13:9b-10 You shall love your neighbor as yourself. Love does no wrong to a neighbor, therefore love is the fulfilling of the law.

14. PARALYZED

The mid 1930's were hot and dry, accompanied by fires and smoke. Many days the sun was only a glow in the smoke. Pastures and crops dried up. We even cut down trees so the cattle could eat the leaves.

Dad rented a vacated 880 farm for pasture, a mile and a half from our home. Then in 1938 he bought the Berg place, 80 acres just a half mile a way (60 acres pasture with permission to fence in another 40 acres) to supplement our Pasture need for 35 head of cattle.

I was 12 years old and along with my brother and sisters (as they were able), was assigned the job of getting the cattle, via the county road, from our barn yard to the Berg place every morning and home again in the evening.

One time as Ken and I were walking home on opposite sides of the road, a car approached and Ken, perhaps with my urging, decided to cross to my side. About half way he saw the car bearing down on him and froze, trying to decide to retreat or continue. Thankfully I was able to grab him and pull him to safety.

Years later I found myself standing next to Billy Graham and George Beverly Shea, like my brother on the road; I froze and couldn't think of a thing to say.

What will it be like when we stand before the King of Kings and the Lord of Lords? I believe we will have a tremendous freedom to praise and thank Him for His redeeming grace. Hallelujah and Amen will be spontaneous as we glory in His presence and explore the delicacies He has prepared for us!

I Cor. 2:9 Eye nor ear has seen or heard all that God has prepared for those who love Him.

15. SALT

Ralph, the youngest of all my uncles and aunts, was 4 years older than I. We did a lot of things together, Ralph and I, some of them best be forgotten, some hilarious and some just good clean fun.

Grandpa and Grandma lived in Mora, Minnesota, and I was spending the weekend with Ralph. He was an energetic 15 year old and decided we should fish the Snake River, which was about a mile west of town.

We would start at the bridge and fish the river north. We wouldn't need to take lunch with us because at noon we could cook the fish we had caught and after lunch we would swim a little and fish the river back to the bridge. That was the plan.

We removed our shoes and socks and hid them in some bushes. Ralph laughed as I took my shoes off because he said I was standing in a poison ivy patch – nice guy, eh? I never did get poison ivy, no thanks to him.

Ralph had some matches in his pocket so when we heard the noon whistle in town we built a fire on a little island in the river and cooked our fish. That's when we discovered, you need salt!!! Needless to say the fish tasted terrible and to make matters worse, while we fixed our fish, a turtle took the stringer with the rest of our fish.

Now salt is a relatively cheap substance and it doesn't take much to make things very tasty so when Jesus said, "You are the salt of the earth," maybe we should sprinkle some of it around.

Matthew 5:13 You are the salt of the earth; but if the salt has become tasteless, how can it be made salty again? It is no longer good for anything, except to be thrown out and trampled underfoot by men.

16. SANITIZED

Warning, the contents of this story may be offensive to sensitive stomachs.

I grew up on a farm six miles northwest of Mora, Minnesota. We milked cows, fed chickens, raised pigs and grew crops - hay, corn, oats, and sometimes rye, barley, and flax. We did most things the hard way, by hand. We carried water from a shallow well for household use. Some of us took a bath once a week, others waited for spring. We mowed hay with horses, raked with a dump rake, shocked it, loaded and stacked it. Then in the cold of winter, we dragged it out of the stack, fed the cows, shoveled the manure and spread it on the field, all by hand. Things were simple too, we had few governmental rules and if cleanliness is next to godliness, by today's standards we would have gotten an "F". The fact is, if the rules for cleanliness today are unconditional, we would have all died young.

When I was a kid, I never heard the word, "Milk Parlor". Milk machines were rare. Dad installed one the day I was sworn into the Army. When I arrived in Camp Fannin, Texas for basic training I wrote the folks, "Now we know who was doing most of the milking." Milking by hand back then was not even close to sanitary by today's standards. We wiped the cow's udder with our hand, squirted a little milk in our hands to lubricate the teats and went to work. It mattered not if a little of the liquid on our hands dripped into the pail – don't even think about mastitis clots. We had a strainer on the cream-can that strained out the straw and other visible kinds of crud.

Then the Creameries, probably by government intervention, began to demand cleaner milk. We had to buy special cloth filters to fasten inside the strainer to capture smaller particles of foreign matter. Then, monthly, we received the results of their filtering, a quarter sized piece of filter on a small card with our grade. We were pleased to learn that we were among the most sanitary – AA - and among the top in our county regarding the amount of product produced.

I'm glad for sanitation rules. The value of pasteurization and homogenization is still being debated, and I still like a good glass of cold whole milk, even if some want to call it raw. I personally believe that the measures employed for cleanliness today are often extreme and destroy bacteria necessary to maintain a natural God given immunity.

The Pharisees were good at cleaning the outside of the cup. They ran everything though their own strainer, removing the visible crud, without noticing the crud that collected in their hearts and disqualified them from earning an AA grade necessary to pass the spiritual filtering process of God. The milk of the word is pure, not to be poured into filthy containers. Both the Lord Jesus and The Apostle Paul said, "Clean out the old leaven." The Psalmist David prayed, "Create in me a clean heart O' Lord." Spiritually, Jesus said, it's not what goes into our mouths but what comes out that defiles. What comes out of our mouths, comes from our heart, and reflects what we have been storing in the warehouse of our hearts. The true filter and only cleansing agent is found in:

I John 1:7 If we walk in the light as He is in the light, we have fellowship with one another, and the blood of Jesus his Son cleanses us from all sin."

Seven Gruver sisters (Dad chose the right one
to be my mom – the one on the right)

17. DAD

My Dad was uneducated but far from being stupid. He was taken out of school in the third grade because of violent headaches, but was permitted to take the state board exams with his class at the end of the eighth grade and received the highest score in the class.

He was the youngest steam engineer in the State of Minnesota, receiving his license at the age of 22. I thought my dad was the best horse-man, the best farmer, the best truck driver, the best steam engineer, the best carpenter, plumber, and mechanic. He could do them all well. He was the best dad a fellow could ever have. You wouldn't be surprised at all if I told you that I loved my dad, would you?

I tried to be like my dad as I grew to manhood and pleasing him was the epitome of success.

Along the way I met my Heavenly Father. My dad had been a good example for me but there were many things dad couldn't do that my Heavenly Father could. There were many things my dad didn't know but my Heavenly Father did. There were many things my dad didn't understand but my Heavenly Father did.

Dad is with my Heavenly Father now and its wonderful to remember him but when I met Jesus, God, my Heavenly Father's Son, He gave me permission to become a member of His Father's family. You wouldn't be surprised if I told you I love my Father in Heaven, would you?

1 John 4:9 By this the love of God was manifested in us, that God has sent His only begotten Son into the world so that we might live through Him.

Family in front of the home place
Dad, Ken, Mom, Verly and Elaine. I was in the 123rd infantry

18. SOMETHING TO DO

People don't visit each other like we did when I was a kid. We often climbed into the old 1930 Chandler, after the cows had been milked, the milk separated, the pigs fed, and drove to a neighbors to share the evening with them, often unannounced.

One time the George Salmonson family came for a visit. The adults visited in the house while we kids played "Blind Man's Bluff" in the yard. As darkness began to settle in that evening, mom turned on the lights in the house. My brother Ken had gone in the house for a drink of water, and I heard dad say, "Tell Roger to start the plant. Our farm, one of the few with electricity, had a 32 volt Delco generator and a bank of batteries that demanded frequent recharging. Ken came out and joined in the game, but said nothing. Later Dad and George came out side and were walking around the yard when Dad said, "Roger, go start the plant." I responded immediately, "Kenny never told me." Everyone laughed and I, red-faced, ducked into the milk house and started the plant.

I have often been asked what kind of farm land we had in central Minnesota. My response is, "You could afford to farm it, if you had a job in town." Dad was a carpenter so until my brother and I were old enough to handle the chores, we had hired men. Those were tough times. I remember young men offering their service for room and board. Hired men came in all sizes generally 16-25 years of age, most of them were good workers but their ability and motivation varied. Some of them were social square pegs. Some were smart and personable, while others were mentally challenged. Some were like me, needing a definite assignment, others saw the walk that needed shoveling, the floor that need to be swept, or the shop bench that needed to be put in order.

Over the years I have come to understand that those men actually represented a cross section of the human family. Jim struggled with simple tasks and never saw anything to do beyond what he was told. Milton saw weeds to chop, feed to grind, multiple ways to be helpful. Bill, perhaps the best hired man we ever had, stole the neighbor's tools and there are the Rogers who procrastinate, plead ignorance and wait for further instructions.

In my years of pastoral ministry I have seen those life styles repeated over and over. I have been with folks who attend Bible classes but never ask a question, or offer a contribution. I've heard folks complain about dust on the piano and the custodian who left it there. It never entered their mind that they could use a dust cloth. "Nobody told me" –"I didn't know" – "that's their job"—are clichés unworthy of those who claim to be members of the body of Christ. We ought to say "How can I help?" "Do you have a dust cloth?" So look around, discover a need, and in the name of Jesus, do an intentional deed of kindness.

James 2:26 "Faith without works is dead."

19. THANKS

My earliest instruction was one word, "No." They did such a good job it took more than twice as long to get me to say, "Yes." The next lesson, mom and dad, grandparents, and about a dozen aunts were determined to make sure I learned, following fast on the heels of the first, two words, "Thank you." Thanks, what a nice, polite word. It would do us all a lot of good to practice using it more often.

We raised Holstein cattle on the farm but even though they were pure Holstein, one of our good cows had a red and white calf. Being quite imaginative, we named her Reddy. Dad planned to ship her as veal, but that didn't work out so we had a red and white Holstein cow that turned out to be an excellent milk cow, birthing many good black and white calves. Reddy had problems calving, so dad, after the vet showed him what to do, worked with her in delivery. Reddy responded by adopting Dad as her special friend, not to be shared. Whenever we worked around the cattle it was okay, unless Dad was there, then Reddy chased us, including the dog, out of the barn yard.

Dad, mom (kids, as we were able) milked 16 cows, morning and evening, the old fashioned way, by hand, the cows assigned to us. The cows stood on a platform, half facing east and half west with a wide aisle in the middle. Dad and I often milked directly across the aisle from each other. Every time dad finished the cow, prior to Reddy, I noticed Reddy put her head back through the stanchion, move over, and moo ever so softly. Then when dad finished milking her, she repeated the same action. I said, "Dad, she's saying please and thank you."

Wilma worked for 20 plus years in the dietary department of rest homes. I recall her often commenting about old people who demanded, "Give me the salt, bring me a drink, pick up my fork." We spend quite a bit of time at the Senior Center here in Stromsburg and often hear, "Get me a cup of coffee, give me a ride home." It seems some have forgotten those early lessons when they were taught to say, "Tell the nice man thank you."

Saying thanks ought to be said even if only as a perfunctory response, though it's certainly much better when it's a genuine "thank you" from the heart. Saying thanks has the power to lift the veil of discouragement, bring sunlight on a cloudy day, and bless a sad heart. When we are truly grateful we fashion a bond of loving kindness with our neighbor and please the Lord at the same time.

We can learn a lot from a red cow who with a soft "moo" blessed our hearts at milking time, morning and evening, everyday, all year long.

I Thessalonians 5:18 Give thanks in all circumstances; for this is the will of God in Christ Jesus for you.

20. HARVEST TIME

Growing up on the family farm, I learned that making a living is always subordinate to living good.

Our income for living was mainly derived from selling milk, eggs, pigs, veal calves, crops, and off the farm work (carpentry or custom work).

Harvest was a small window of opportunity to reap the fruit of our spring and summer labor. The little window, late August to early October, was of extreme value to us, requiring immediate attention and our best efforts. All other activities at harvest time became secondary, except the spiritual – prayer, worship and godly living always had jurisdiction over making a living.

Harvest demanded preparations: getting the binder ready, checking the rollers, canvas aprons, roller chains, sharpening the sickle, replacing broken sections, checking the knotter, kicker, and carrier.

There were limitations, however, beyond our control: the crop was too green or wet, the sweat (curing the grain in the shock), and of course the threshers had their own schedule. And unforeseen things like the flu, injuries, death, and bad weather could stop or delay the harvest.

So it's easy for me to understand what the Lord Jesus meant when He said the harvest is ready but there aren't enough laborers.

There is a little window of time to bring in a very valuable harvest, not just oats, wheat, or corn, but a harvest of souls. So pray forth laborers remembering that you too are a laborer, so get ready and get to work!

Matthew 9:37-38 (NASB) Then He said* to His disciples, "The harvest is plentiful, but the workers are few. [38] *"Therefore beseech the Lord of the harvest to send out workers into His harvest.*

Grandpa, George Burke, surrounded by great grandkids:
Philip, Doris, Roxane, Timothy and Marjorie
(Our kids called him the "funny grandpa" – he was
not that mellow when I was growing up)

21. TROUBLE ON THE FARM

There was a lot of haying to do in 1937. Dad was in the University Hospital in Minneapolis trying to discover what caused his frequent headaches and dizzy spells; a problem that had, by doctor's orders, exempted him from school since the third grade. My uncles, Goodwin and Lowell, enlisted my brother and I (I was almost 11 and Ken 8 ½) to help put up the hay on four farms. We were to keep the loads level and tramped, while our uncles pitched the hay from shocks onto the hayrack. Goodie was 33, married and in charge. Lowell was 21 and ornery, if he found a snake or some Canadian Thistles he always tried to throw them on top of us. It was a long hot summer.

Dad was home, without a diagnosis, other than speculation that he had a nagging wife, or some other psychological problem. The lack of milk cooling facilities had evolved into a cooperative effort between Grandpa Burke, Uncle Alfred and dad taking turns hauling the cream to town. One day, early in 1938, grandpa didn't stop to pick up our cream. We thought he may have run out of snuff, which often caused an ugly reaction, but we were soon to learn that the problem was bigger than that. The family almost immediately chose up sides and things progressed from bad to worse. Uncle Goodwin stuck with Dad while most of the other family members were for Grandpa.

That year grandpa was selling the farm to Alfred and auctioning off all the farm machinery, cattle, and produce. Dad owned a lot of the equipment in partnership with Grandpa and we discovered, via the grapevine, that grandpa was planning to sell Dad's part on the auction. Needless to say, the pressure didn't help Dad's nerves, but the day of the sale, a neighbor, Frank Sonbuckner, cautioned everyone he knew at the sale not to bid against my dad. The result was that we purchased all we needed at a very reasonable price. The steam engine and thresh machine was on our property so they couldn't sell them.

I remember threshing on our farm in October 1938, and Grandpa tried to shut us down. Uncle Goodwin leapt from the top of the separator (it seemed to me) to the ground and ordered his dad, (Grandpa) off the place.

Five years went by and a Methodist preacher (bless his heart) convinced Grandpa that he had to ask Dad for forgiveness. I'll never forget the evening Grandpa asked Dad to forgive him as they cried and hugged each other. It was a very emotional time at our house. We never did find out what Grandpa's problem was, but it was awfully good to have the family back together.

Dad returned to the University Hospital in 1939 and was sent home, presumably to die. Uncle Paul Gruver was to bring him home when a flier, advertising the new Minneapolis Chiropractic Hospital, was tossed on their porch. Dad thought they were quacks, but Uncle Paul said, "You know they sent you home to die; what other choice do you have?"

So Dad was admitted to the hospital by a young doctor and placed in a bed opposite the admissions desk. Later he heard the doctor being scolded for admitting one so close to death. Their diagnosis, "His neck bone had been dislocated at birth, and was over by his ear." Dad responded well to the treatment and returned home a new man. He lived for over 40 years after that and never had another violent headache.

James 1:12 Blessed is a man who perseveres under trial; for once he has been approved, he will receive the crown of life which the Lord has promised to those who love Him.

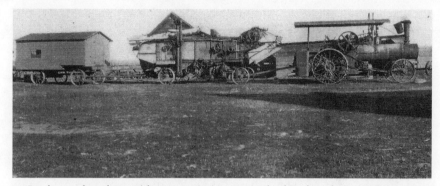

Let's go threshing (the steam engine with the threshing machine,
sleeping shack and generally and tank wagon, were familiar
sights in October and November every year. The fuel was mainly
stump roots, which each farmer was required to furnish)

22. THE STEAMER

A steam engine can be identified by smell, sound, smoke, its whistle, and of course, by sight. That 75 horse J. I. Case steam engine and 36X58 threshing machine sitting in Grandpa's yard occupies my earliest memories. Grandpa and Dad owned it together. My Dad was the engineer and Grandpa was the Separator man.

I remember with delight, crawling up into the cab of that giant engine in the twilight of the evening to pull the whistle cord to see if there was enough steam to send that unique piercing sound echoing across the fields and woods.

The threshing season was from October until early December, and, except on Sundays, I seldom saw Dad. Dad never worked on Sunday. Six days a week he left home before I got up and returned after I had gone to bed.

We rented the 850 acre Chamberlain farm, a mile and a half southwest of our farm, in the early thirties, mainly for pasture. We also used the barn on that property for milking.

One time, Dad was threshing at the Bronson Farm, 6 miles south of us, as the crow flies. That evening Grandpa Gruver, (mom's dad) hauled us, along with the milk pails and ten gallon cream cans, to the farm. Mom expected Dad to come and help finish the milking and take us home.

I remember it was a cold evening and after Mom finished milking we sat on the barn floor and hugged the ten gallon cream cans trying to keep warm. We heard the steam engine whistle about nine that evening, signaling the end of threshing for that day. It was a very dark night (no electricity) and nearly ten, before Dad finally arrived to rescue us.

Dad from childhood struggled with terrible headaches, which were now causing fainting and balance control problems, so in 1939 we sold the steam engine and threshing machine.

My Uncle Goodwin delivered the engine driving it some 20 miles to the Zimple Sawmill at McGrath, Minnesota. When he passed the Lowell School, District 24, where I was an eighth grader, he saw me in the window and pulled the cord for several short warbles of the whistle.

I remember tears rolling down my cheeks — it was a sad day. Now I look back and remember with great delight and thankfulness.

2 Corinthians 4:18 While we look not at the things which are seen, but at the things which are not seen; for the things which are seen are temporal, but the things which are not seen are eternal.

23. BALANCED

The Great Armistice Blizzard, November 11, 1940, hit while my folks were in town (Mora, Minnesota) shopping. Snow piled up quickly driven by gale force winds and our driveway was totally blocked by huge snow drifts.

Through the garage window I saw a propeller I had built years before, spinning like crazy then break apart (I had never seen the prop spin before) that's when I saw the car being towed across the field by my uncle with a team of horses. Snow billowed up and off the headlights, the harness tugs were like fiddle strings, but praise the Lord, the folks made it home (144 souls perished in that storm).

Back to the propeller – I had simply taken a couple of lathes, fastened them like a prop on a plane, and nailed them on top of a fence post. It wasn't centered, or balanced, and the prop had no pitch. At age 7 I wasn't bothered about details. The prop didn't function and its predictable end was disaster!

I share this because so many in our world, so many families, break up when the winds of adversity blow. They are out of balance and with out proper pitch. They survive for a while when winds begin to blow but soon begin to spin out of control and blow up!

What we need in our homes and in our personal lives is what we can have in Jesus Christ. When He is at the center He adjusts the pitch, keeps us balanced so we can handle the strongest gale force winds and win.

Romans 8:35-37 Who will separate us from the love of Christ? Will tribulation, or distress, or persecution, or famine, or nakedness, or peril, or sword? [37] *in all these things we overwhelmingly conquer through Him who loved us.*

24. A MAN

I was 16 when I read the 1916 edition of "When A Man's A Man," the story of a city boy from the east, half owner of a ranch out west, who decided to go, anonymously, to test his manhood as a ranch hand.

Men are fascinated with brawn and think ladies are too. A 6'7" fleet footed 340 lb football player sacking the quarterback, or a 5'8" broad shouldered brute lifting a truck tire over the side of a pickup box with one hand are the subject of many a conversation.

I remember my uncles trying to lift the rear wheel of the old Wallace tractor. My brother Ken and I put a belt under the scale and over our shoulders to test our lifting strength. Torval, a bachelor neighbor, could drive a 16 penny spike held in the palm of his hand through a one inch pine board. Men want to be the man's man, run faster, jump higher, bench press more, and never be a 98 pound weakling.

But let me tell you about the real man's man. His name is Jesus. He abandoned his power as God in order to be a man among us. He never flinched in the face of danger, never backed away from thieves, or angry mobs. He cared for the suffering, the poor and loved little children. And finally, though he could have called 10,000 angels, he faced the cross, took our place, bore our condemnation, and died alone.

Jesus conquered death and unveiled God's plan for us all. It is in Jesus that men find the strength and courage — the manliness they want to encourage in all the boys who follow them seeking after their own manhood.

Jeremiah 29:11 I know the plans that I have for you, declares the Lord, plans for welfare and not for calamity to give you a future and a hope.

25. FRIENDS

I rode the bus six miles all four years of high school. Clyde Dalbey, a year or two older than I, rode the same bus but got on some eight miles ahead of me. I admired his six foot, 180 pounds (I'm guessing) of bulging muscles. I was five foot eight and barely 100 pounds.

If I went to church, it would have been the same country church he attended. The bus ride, however, is where we connected and became friends forever. So when Clyde invited me to the weekly youth meetings at church, because of my respect for him, I accepted the invitation to the youth meetings and also began attending church.

The result of his invitation and my decision was a renewed relationship to Jesus Christ. After a while we formed a Gospel Team, and contacted several of the rural schools asking permission to use the school to hold a preaching service with singing and testimonies. It was a lot of fun and a great spiritual experience. All of this convinced me to follow the Lord in baptism and to join the church.

Uncle Sam interrupted all of that and I was inducted into the Army. It was nearly two years later when I came home to discover that my friend Clyde was no longer active in the church. Our Pastor, Paul Lundgren, told me Clyde had been playing cards, etc. Saturday nights and getting home so late he didn't get up in time to attend church. Then, before I had opportunity to talk to him, he was drafted.

I prayed and wept before the Lord for my friend Clyde for a long time, then the Lord impressed me to write a letter, reminding him of the joy and delight we had shared together serving in the name of Jesus. The Lord used that letter, among other things, to bring Clyde back into the fold.

Years later He was the Pastor of our home church and I was asked to share in the service. That was my opportunity to thank him publically for his touch on my life. He responded similarly with thanks to me — it was a hugging hallelujah party that morning at the Hillman Baptist Church. Praise the Lord with thanksgiving for my friend, Clyde!

Clyde lives with his wife Alyce in Mora, MN. We are still best of friends and one of these days we're going to get together and really celebrate our friendship around the throne of God!

Proverbs 17:17 A friend loves at all times.

26. HE MEANT ME

English Lit class in high school was boring, and I was day dreaming when I realized the teacher was asking me a question and I didn't have the foggiest idea what she had asked. I tried to duck, to get the fellow next to me to answer, but the teacher meant me and wouldn't let me off the hook until I finally admitted my reckless lack of concern.

Life contains a series of glitches, distractions like that; significant moments missed because we were flying solo in our own fantasy world.

I remember at VBS I prayed with one of the teachers and asked Jesus to come into my heart. I believe He did but I never gave Him much space, I was too preoccupied with my own agenda; hunting, fishing and having fun occupied my time and I didn't know what God was saying.

It was just after my 18th birthday that I heard the question and I knew it was the Lord. "Will you let me be the Lord of your life?" He asked. That night I admitted my sinfulness, my selfish preoccupation, and surrendered to His Lordship, asking Jesus to occupy the throne in my life.

I began to meditate on His Word and pray over the path He wanted me to walk. My call to pastoral ministry didn't come like a bolt of lightning, but by paying attention, and living obediently the Lord Jesus directed my path until I knew.

When I paid attention it wasn't long before I knew that Jesus, God the Son really meant me and I was called to preach the Gospel!

2 Peter 1:10 Therefore, brethren, be all the more diligent to make certain about His calling and choosing you; for as long as you practice these things, you will never stumble.

27. PHARISEES

My earliest memories of how to live Christian is explained by the old saying, "Don't drink, smoke, dance, or chew, or run around with girls who do."

I remember the sharp rejection of: a proposal to let the young people dance in the church basement, a heated argument when a family bought a nice gold cross and candles for the communion table, and again when a Sunday school teacher handed out bracelets with an inscription to help them remember to obey Jesus. We didn't roller skate because the rink was in the Fish Lake dance pavilion. The bottom line was there will be no idolatry or appearance of evil in our church!

It's easier to check up on yourself and appear righteous if you have rules. Rules help you see the flaws in others. You can shape up a congregation by applying the rules — Pharisees play by the rules.

I can't remember when I began to realize that obedience to rules, whether written or oral, are a far cry from David's confession, "I love Thy Law." Or following Jesus words, "He who has my commandments and keeps them, he it is who loves me." Or "This is my commandment that you love one another, just as I have loved you."

I know that God's law has never been repealed. I also know it's my relationship with Him through His Son that enables my behavior to yield in obedience to His law of love.

I never have to check a list of things I should do to love my wife. I never ask her if I have to love her. My love for her has never been viewed as a duty. Law is only necessary when love runs out. My Christianity does not result from what I do, what I do results from who I am in relationship to the Lord Jesus Christ.

1 John 3:16 We know love by this, that He laid down His life for us; and we ought to lay down our lives for the brethren.

28. THE WELL

We moved to the farm six miles north of Mora, Minnesota in 1928, and for the next 15 years all the water needed for the family had to be carried some 150 feet from the well. So during summer vacation 1943 Dad decided to dig a well.

We gathered the equipment: a tripod with a pulley in the apex, some rope, a hook, a five gallon bucket, a couple of shovels, a pick, and a 16 pound hammer. The plan was to dig next to the house and run a pipe through the wall into the basement where the pump and supply tank would be located with a galvanized pipe running straight up into the kitchen with a not so fancy faucet on top of it.

The first part was easy, taking turns with pick and shovel and hammer to break up an occasional rock. The bucket became necessary as the hole deepened to remove dirt lower the tools.

Twenty feet down Dad said, "I need the hammer." Placing the hammer in the bucket and hanging it on the hook I began lowering the 21 lbs (bucket and hammer) then I noticed the bail of the bucket was on the point of the hook and turning. "Look out!" I yelled. Dad looked up and the bucket hit him on the forehead. I thought I had killed my Dad, who went to his knees but remained conscious. He was able to tie the rope around himself so that Mom and I could pull him up out of the well.

I confess I did some very intense praying that day and God who is faithful took care of our need. Dad was okay and at about 22 feet we had good running water in our house — praise the Lord!

John 4:13-14 Jesus said to her, "Everyone who drinks of this water will thirst again; [14] but whoever drinks of the water that I will give him shall never thirst; but the water that I will give him will become in him a well of water springing up to eternal life."

Hillman Baptist Church – dedicated in 1926, became our church in the 1940's. It was located in the country, about 12 miles north of Mora, MN. It nearly closed in the fifties, but grew and has gone through 3 building additions.

29. INSTRUMENTS OF JOY

The great Violinist Itzhak Perlman was playing at the Avery Fisher Hall, Lincoln Center, N.Y. City, as he began a string on his violin broke. He modulated, recomposed, changed notes and finished to a standing ovation. He said, "Sometimes it is good to find out how much you can do with what you've got left."

Most church musicians are not as talented as that, but I remember Phylliss Newcomer singing a solo at a funeral when the power went off and the organ died; Phylliss never missed a note while the Organist moved to the piano. Most church musicians are generous, caring folks who are willing to share the measure of talent the Lord has given them.

One such person was Molly Dalbey, a plain ordinary gracious lady, who played the old pedal type organ for the Hillman Baptist church. Molly was far from professional. She made mistakes, getting the wrong page, skipping a verse, but she kept playing. She was dependable, durable, always wore a smile and probably the only one who could play the old pump organ enabling us to sing the great hymns of the church.

The organ bench Molly sat on was about a chair and a quarter high and was becoming very loose jointed. The trustees had been warned but took no action. So it was on a Sunday in 1944, Molly positioned herself on the bench, pumped air into the bellows of the organ, raised her hands to strike the first chord and with a loud crash, the bench collapsed! Molly laid full length on the platform while pandemonium broke loose in the church. Trustees and Deacons, running this way and that, one helping Molly up, a couple picking up pieces of the shattered bench, another looking for a stool high enough to replace the bench. Molly, with her index finger in her mouth, tried to tuck in behind the organ. Meanwhile the congregation was bursting their innards, wanting to roar with laughter, but out of politeness and respect was trying to hold it in. Molly was terribly embarrassed, but as soon as the platform was cleared and a suitable stool was found, she resumed her place, pumped the organ and the worship service was underway.

I thank God for those precious people, humble servants of the Lord, who like Molly, share, not to perform, but to minister. Though few are the times they receive recognition, they continue to praise the Lord, thankful for the opportunity to use the gifts they were given to glorify the Lord Jesus.

One might think the organ or the piano was the instrument, but the real instrument is the person who humbly week after week with little fan-fare share their gifts. These People, thus blest of the Lord, are the true instruments and thus blest have the privilege of spreading the joy around.

Nehemiah 8:10 -The worship service was over and the people instructed to go and have a great dinner, and send gifts to the needy, for he says, "The Joy of the Lord is your strength."

30. MIRACLE IN A HAYFIELD

My cousin Duane and I registered for the draft together in 1944 just before our 18th birthday. Hoping for a farm deferment Uncle Paul (Duane's dad), anticipating the event, had purchased machinery, cows, horses, and rented the Luloff place (640 acres, a mile from our farm). He worked out an agreement with my dad to help with the farming, so Duane (age 18) moved from Minneapolis to Kanabec County, Minnesota to become a farmer.

That's why one mid-afternoon in July, 1944, we were a ½ mile south of his house haying. Duane was raking, I pulling a buck-rake with the tractor, my dad and brother, Ken helping load. It was coffee time so the guys got on the loaded buck-rake to ride to the house, as I released the clutch the far horse began making a fuss; he had kicked at a fly and his foot was over the belly strap.

Duane and Ken ran to his aid, Duane over the tongue, Ken around the back of the rake, when suddenly the horses reared up, pulling the small sapling anchor up by the roots. Duane jumped but one leg went through the breaching. He grabbed the back straps of the harness and was suspended upside down. The horses, now out of control, raced down the field with Duane repeatedly having his head and shoulders rammed into the meadow sod only to be catapulted again and again high into the air. Finally, knocked unconscious, he lay in a heap on the ground.

Ken ran after the horses, Dad to Duane, and I followed with the load of hay. I could see Duane on the ground, blood trickling from his mouth, eyes, and ears. "Is he alive," I asked? Dad stood up and replied, "I don't think so." I leaped from the tractor and kneeling by the buck rake cried out unashamedly to the Lord for Duane's life, as I prayed I heard a raspy breath – he was alive!

We rushed him 6 miles to Doctor Bossart's office in Mora. The nurse, pointing to a cot said, "The Doctor will be with you in a minute." Doc was fitting glasses on an elderly woman so we waited and waited and waited until I was so angry I had to go for a walk to cool down.

To make a long story short, Duane had bruises but no broken bones and was back at work a few days later. Do I believe in miracles? You bet! The doctor may delay but Jesus will be there on time all the time!

Jeremiah 33:3 Call to Me and I will answer you, and I will tell you great and mighty things, which you do not know.

31. GET ON THE PLANK

It was a nice spring Saturday in early April 1944, my brother and I were about to do what we did every Saturday from October until mid April, clean the barn. We put the manure on the fields the old fashioned way, spreading one fork full at a time. We harnessed the horses and hooked up to the big rubber tired wagon. The yard behind the barn was much too muddy so I backed the wagon up to the front door of the barn. Ken brought the plank we used as a ramp for the wheel barrow and laid it across the threshold of the door.

I positioned the wagon and walked to the door and noticed Ken was standing on the inside end of the plank. I couldn't resist, I leaped, and with everything I had, hit my end of the plank; looking up I saw my wide-eyed brother's face through the window above the door. He landed with a few words of rebuke; then the light bulb went on in our heads, why not make a trampoline? The modern trampoline was invented in 1934, but we had never seen one. The word is actually Spanish for a diving board, and that's what we had in mind.

We finished cleaning the barn and went scouting for material to build a trampoline. We found a rough sawn Elm or Oak plank 2" X 14" and 18 feet long. I don't recall asking Dad's permission, but he never complained. We found a chunk of wood 18 inches long and about 16 inches in diameter, ran some twenty penny spikes through the middle of the plank into the chunk of wood, and we had ourselves a trampoline.

All that was left now was to learn how to ride that thing. We had to learn how to help the board get us airborne. If your knees weren't locked at take-off the board hit you in your posterior hard and you didn't get any lift. The second thing was balance. I remember being at the top of my ascent when my brother, realizing he was off balance hollered, "Wait a minute." I of course descended immediately and sent him into the weeds. We also had to learn how to hit the board straight and hard by straightening your legs as you contacted the board to give the maximum lift to the catapult end of the board. Land stiff legged when the other guy wasn't ready and you got a big shock the full length of your spine.

We practiced long and hard to perfect our technique. Eventually both of us were able to sail high enough to look over the top of the electric wires that went from the yard light to the peak of the milk house. That was higher than standing on the top of a big hayrack load of hay.

The point of my story is simply this, for my brother and me to achieve anything near a satisfactory result we had to work in harmony. We both had to give and receive, share the ups and downs of the trampoline experience.

That's a lesson worth remembering for professing Christians. Brothers and sisters in Christ must learn to forgive, or to ask forgiveness, and never refuse to get back on the plank. It really hurts when you land alone with no one on the other end of the plank to cushion the blow, and when no one is there you don't get airborne at all.

Proverbs 11:24 One gives freely, yet grows richer; another withholds what he should give and only suffers want.

32. BAPTIZED

My cousin Marjorie and I were baptized on April 10, 1945 in the Stanchfield Baptist Church, 30 some miles south of the Hillman Baptist church where we were attending.

The Hillman Church, not having a baptistery, often used a river near the church, but in April the water was much too cold and time was crucial as I was 4 weeks from being inducted into the Army. So Pastor Paul Lundgren made arrangements with the Stanchfield Church and we were to meet him there about 7 P.M.

Not having a car I planned to use Dad's 1937 Chrysler. The evening of the baptism Dad worked late and I was frustrated waiting, and Pastor Paul, waiting at the church 30 miles away was about to give up on us.

There were about 16 from our youth group and no adults, other than Pastor Paul, that witnessed our baptism. I often wondered why my parents or some of the adults from the church chose not to come, until I remembered during the Second World War gas and tires rationing were serious restrictions on all travel.

I shall never forget, in spite of the frustrations, how Pastor Paul led us in a simple gospel service and then baptized Marjorie and me. We had followed, in obedience, the steps of our Lord, going down into the waters and coming up out of the waters depicting our death, burial, and resurrection.

I didn't understand a lot of the theology but I knew I loved the Lord Jesus and had been obedient in following Him. It was a great Day!

Romans 6:4 (NASB) ***Therefore we have been buried with Him through baptism into death, so that as Christ was raised from the dead through the glory of the Father, so we too might walk in newness of life.***

33. REPORT FOR DUTY

Uncle Sam notified me to report to Fort Snelling for active duty on the 9th of May 1945. I knew baptism also carried with it the responsibility of reporting for duty as a member of a body of which Christ was the head. Having been baptized on the 10th of April with a departure date set for May 9th there wasn't much time to report.

So on Sunday May 6, 1945 Pastor Paul asked me to give a brief testimony of my faith and with the chairman of the Board of Deacons recommendation I was received into the membership of the Hillman Baptist Church.

There was a lot of loving support from the church, both young and old. They had invested in me by preparing me to live for Jesus. I had no idea what was ahead of me but I was confident that they would be faithful in prayer on my behalf, regardless of my destination and I would not be disappointed!

Upon completion of my tour of duty with the Army I began preparing for the Gospel Ministry, the church encouraged me by issuing a license to preach the Gospel. It was their way of saying "We believe God has called you and we are behind you."

On July 30, 1949 Pastor Paul officiated at my marriage to Wilma Trupe. Wilma's family also belonged to the Hillman Church. Wilma and I remained members of that church until 1954 when we transferred our membership to First Baptist of Two Harbors.

Years of preparation passed, and having reported for duty at the Calvary Baptist Church – Cambridge, NE – in July of 1964, I was Ordained on the 9th of May 1969 and Pastor Paul preached my ordination sermon.

I look forward to a great reunion day when with all those folks from Hillman Baptist Church we gather around the throne of God. Oh, what a day that will be!

Revelation 2:10b (NASB) Be faithful until death, and I will give you the crown of life.

34. BLESSED

The poster said, "Uncle Sam wants you!" The letter said it was a recommendation from my neighbors and the newspaper said I had been "called up". That's the way it was in 1945. During my military service I felt called of God to pastoral ministry and my Pastor Paul Lundgren and church family agreed.

My preparation began September 1947 at Bethel College, St. Paul, MN. Pastor Paul encouraged the church to grant me a license to preach and in 1948 they asked me to Pastor a satellite ministry of the Church. I prayed fervently for God's will - then as I drove the 14 miles north from Mora, Minnesota, to our rural Hillman Baptist Church, an audible voice said, "To the work!" I have never heard that voice since, though I've wished many times I could, but I accepted the voice as God's sign and became the pastor of the "Little Ann Sunday School and Church".

The church had a solid core of believers willing to work with a naïve untrained preacher and the Lord blessed that ministry, a number were saved and others rededicated their lives to Christ. My time at Little Ann became part of my preparation for pastoral ministry, sharpening the reality of God's call and claim on my life.

I had no idea that wrapped up in God's call to Little Ann was a young lady, a senior in high school, who would become my wife. We look back today after more than 60 years together at multiplied blessing, abundant and over flowing, poured out by our loving Lord. Obedience to God's call always brings blessing.

James 1:25 But one who looks intently at the perfect law, the law of liberty, and abides by it, not having become a forgetful hearer but an effectual doer, this man will be blessed in what he does.

Roger Burke and Wally Bismark, taken in Takarazuka, Japan. They took Basic Training at Camp Fannin, near Tyler, Texas, shipped overseas and served together for about six months and have remained the best of friends for the last sixty-five years.

35. WHERE THE POWER IS!

October 23, 1945 as the band played "Going to Take a Sentimental Journey", I departed from Tacoma, Washington, aboard the Admiral Coontz, a 680 foot troop carrier. The Pacific Ocean had just been stirred up by a typhoon and was still quite rough. The storm had dislodged a number of mines that were now floating free. We sank 4 or five of them on our 18 day trip to join the occupation army in Japan. We pulled into the bay at Nagasaki and got stuck in the mud for most of the day. When the ship finally backed out of the mud, the order had arrived that we should go to Nagoya for deployment, thus escaping possible radioactive contamination from the atomic bomb at Nagasaki.

I was stationed just outside of Takarazuka, near Kobe with G Company, the 123rd Infantry, 33rd Division. Our task was to collect all articles related to war and search the area for secret caches of armament. We were charged with security at the compound, a former ball bearing factory, converted to barracks for two companies, and a small airfield. We also searched the area around Biwa, Japan's largest lake near Kyoto. The 33rd was deactivated in January 1946 and the colors sent back to its original home, the Illinois State Guard. We moved in with A Company, downtown Takarazuka, then to temporary barracks with the 310 Bomber Wing, finally assigned to the 81st Signal Service which changed it designation to the 3186$^{th.}$ Later, due to a clerical error, I was transferred permanently to the Air Force.

While stationed with the 3186th I experienced the power of God. I was a very young Christian when I entered the Army. During basic training I was encouraged by the base chaplain and several enlisted men and officers with whom I met for Bible Study. Overseas at this point in time I had never met a chaplain or found a chapel and though I still kept my Bible on an end table by my cot it had been neglected for some time. I made the usual trip to the mess hall for supper and joked around with the guys for awhile before returning to my room. When I entered the room my eyes fastened on the Bible. I reached over and opened it randomly and read Psalm 19:14, "Let the words of my mouth and the meditations of my heart be acceptable in thy sight O Lord, my strength and my redeemer." The verse was like a hammer blow to my head and heart. I fled to an area behind the barracks to pray and weep before the Lord. Repenting of my neglect, I told the Lord that I wanted more than anything else in the world to be acceptable in His sight.

A few days later I received a letter from Grandma Burke.

Dear Roger, I was awakened at two this morning and impressed to pray for you. I don't know what the need is, but I knelt beside the bed and prayed for you. With all my love, Grandma.

I counted the time difference in between Mora, Minnesota and Japan, and it really wasn't a surprise to discover Grandma was praying for me at the exact moment The Holy Spirit convicted me with the Scripture, Psalm 19:14.

Where is the power? Jesus said, "All power is given unto me." He sent the Holy Spirit to convict, guide, strengthen us, and interpret our prayers. The Word of God is powerful, and the prayer of a righteous person has great power. I experienced them all, the power of God, the power of the Holy Spirit, the power of the Word, and Grandma's prayer. That's where the power of God is.

II Cor. 4:7 We have this treasure in jars of clay to show that the surpassing power belongs to God and not to us.

36. FORGIVEN

I was serving in Japan in 1946 with the 5th Army Air Force Headquarters Squadron, 21st Air Service Group, stationed at the Army Air base near Ashia on Kyushu Island about halfway between Nagasaki and Hiroshima – our home away from home.

Everyone looked forward to mail call, even the "Dear John" letters. Many of us, me included, received at least one! I remember one of my Mother's letters telling about our neighbors' boy. The young man grew up on the hill just east of our farm. I knew him when he was still in diapers. Our families visited back and forth quite often and we kids attended the same school.

I remember the day he accidently set fire to a straw pile next to their barn. They didn't have a phone so he ran the nearly half mile to our house to ask us to call the fire department. We watched helplessly as their barn burned to the ground.

He was about 17 years old in 1946 and Mom wrote to tell me they had found him in the middle of the night wandering the road in his pajamas, wringing his hands and crying as he mumbled something about being lost and asking, "How do I get right with God?" Some of the neighbors thought he had lost his mind and might be a threat to the community. As I read the letter I wondered if anyone cared enough to tell him how he could be just before God?

His question was not new. Job and his 3 friends asked it, "How can a man be just with God?" The Lawyer in Luke 10 asked Jesus, "What shall I do to inherit eternal life?"

I hope that whenever the question is asked that someone says, "Jesus is the only way to get right with God".

Romans 5:1 Therefore having been justified by faith, we have peace with God through our Lord Jesus Christ.

Romans 3:26 God is just and the Justifier of all who come to Him.

Romans 8:1 Therefore there is now no condemnation for those who are in Christ Jesus.

37. A FAIR SHARE

Possession may be nine tenths of the law but it doesn't help when you know your sister is wearing your sweater, or your brother borrowed your suit. My parents told me to clean up my room, but I knew my brother was the one who kicked his dirty clothes under the bed and left stuff laying all over the room. I wanted him to take ownership, but not of my stuff.

When my parents reminded me that I was 2 ½ years older than my brother it didn't create unity. It made me aware of my rights. We settled by dividing our room —mine and his!

Personal rights are hard to relinquish. We hear much about "inalienable rights" and being "created equal". The problem is, as with my brother and me, the matter of application – how does one go about getting his/her rights without infringing on the rights of others.

My brother and I became better friends by separation – I to the Army while he stayed on the farm. We finally surrendered our rights and discovered in Jesus the unity we both wanted. We learned to work together, log together, build houses together, hunt together, and raise chickens together without ever once bickering about our rights.

I wrote my brother from Japan in 1945 and enclosed this verse, "Brother's are people you fight with but love more than you could ever say." We didn't always agree, but we loved each other and always looked eagerly forward to every opportunity to be together.

My brother died in 2001 and I miss him, but one day I shall join him in the presence of our Lord Jesus, then we shall glory not in our rights but in our unity.

Philippians 2:2 Make my joy complete by being of the same mind, maintaining the same love, united in spirit, intent on one purpose.

38. PERSPECTIVE

World War II and Halloween 1945 were history. I was in Japan serving in the Occupation Army when I received two letters sharing two perspectives about the CYF (my church youth), Halloween escapade.

The first letter was from one of the girls in the youth group. "We had a lot of fun at your parent's farm", she said, "soaping a few windows and moving machinery". She said, "When your mother turned on the yard light it helped us see what we were doing".

The second letter was from my mother. She had not seen the evening as enjoyable. "I turned on the light" she said, "Hoping to scare them away instead they ran the Seeder tongue (like a drill for planting oats) up against the door to keep me in the house, in fact," she said, "they ran the tongue clear through the storm door". Mom was not a happy camper.

We often struggle with issues, (social, political, theological, whatever) and can't understand the perspective of those on the other side of the Seeder. Preset ideas and pride often keep us from reaching a unified perspective?

If you start when one is in the house and the other behind the Seeder, you'll probably never agree. The answer I believe is in going back to a position prior to the Seeder. What is basic to our relationship is the fundamental truth that existed before Halloween?

The Apostle John wrote the Gospel about 90 AD, after the synoptic Gospels and after Paul's Epistles, putting the need for unanimity in laying the foundation in perspective?

John 1:1-3 (NASB) [1] *In the beginning was the Word, and the Word was with God, and the Word was God.* [2] *He was in the beginning with God.* [3] *All things came into being through Him, and apart from Him nothing came into being that has come into being.*

We must begin at the beginning with a good foundation and never ever presume to build on anything else.

39. DARKNESS

God's first creative act on this empty, formless earth was light. Men may love darkness rather than light when their deeds are evil but Wilma and I love light, in fact our house is seldom totally dark every room has a night light of one sort or another.

Darkness has a way of amplifying things that go bump in the night. It gives eerie shapes to ordinary things and amplifies sounds that create weird images in the mind.

It seemed to me that my tour of guard duty in the army always came in the middle of the night and (with one exception) I was assigned the same post, a two block long el shape with a burning barrel at the end of one leg and a hole in the wall at the backside of camp on the other with a 40 watt light at the corner;

Japan had surrendered in 1945 and my unit, the 123rd Infantry 33rd division set up camp just north-west of Kobe in Takarazuka. Our barracks were in an abandoned Japanese forced labor, Ball-bearing factory.

I accepted the clip of ammo one night from the guard I was relieving and a Thomson-sub Machine gun cut loose on the next post. I could hear the bullets zinging this way and that. Finally a guard came through to say a couple Japanese were trying to break into the Ammunition supply warehouse and were still inside the compound.

Walking my post meant walking into the light or away from it to the hole in the wall at the backside of camp. The walk was cluttered on both sides with old machines, ideal obstacles for surprise attack. So I reasoned walking my post in the dark would be stupid not heroic. Therefore, like any sensible soldier would do, I fixed bayonet, put a round of ammo in the rifle chamber, and backed into the shadow of a building and with my back to the wall stood perfectly still until I was relieved several hours later.

I have had many scary experiences in the dark, most of them products of an over worked mind, but that night in Japan it wasn't my imagination, it was reality and every nerve in my body was on high alert. When the light of dawn replaced the darkness, what unimaginable relief and freedom flooded my being. I love light rather than darkness!

1 John 1:5 This is the message we have heard from Him and announce to you, that God is Light, and in Him there is no darkness at all.

40. MY MAN

Poem written by my mother Geneva Fern (Gruver) Burke in 1947 honoring my 21st birthday.

Just a little while ago you were a little tot,
I used to wash your face and hands and pick you up a lot.
I like to think about those days as mothers only can
But today my little boy today you are a man

I packed away your dresses, your rompers and your suits
And then I packed away your little crocheted baby boots
Yes, packed away, or passed them on to others who were smaller
And every year I watched you grow bigger, stronger, taller

Not long ago you trudged to school then learned to skate and shoot
Sometimes you'd run around and play dressed in your Indian suit
Sometimes you'd peddle down the road and in the river swam
But today, should I be glad or sad to say today you are a man

Your high school days went by too fast
It seemed no time 'til they were past
But you improved as they went by
Combing hair and wearing tie

I know you've been a lot of places that I shall never be
And you've seen a lot of things that I shall never see
I know you've sailed the ocean wide, and lived in far Japan
But then you were my little boy, today you are my man!

Psalm 1:1-3 How blessed is the man who does not walk in the counsel of the wicked, Nor stand in the path of sinners, Nor sit in the seat of scoffers! 2 But his delight is in the law of the Lord, And in His law he meditates day and night. 3 He will be like a tree firmly planted by streams of water, Which yields its fruit in its season And its leaf does not wither; And in whatever he does, he prospers.

41. OUT OF THE PIT

I served my final months of military service overseas on Kyushu Island, Japan with the 5th Air Force's 21st Air Service Command stationed at the Ashiya Army Airbase. The first few months at Ashiya we did not have a Chaplain but seven of us G.I.'s were planning to enter some phase of Christian ministry when we finished our tour of duty, so we took on the Chapel duties – preparing the services, rousting the men out on Sunday morning, and taking turns preaching.

When I finally landed stateside, sensing a solid call to ministry, I was primed to get with it! Encouraged by my church and Pastor, I enrolled at Bethel College in the fall of 1947. — I was as high up the mountain as I had ever been. My expectations were in the clouds, but alas, reality was about to set in and I would suffer a rapid descent to the floor of a deep, ugly crevasse of discouragement.

Problem # 1 – If I had learned how to study in High School, I had forgotten. Problem # 2 – I became the reigning Badminton Champion in the boy's dorm, and lacked the self discipline to say "no" to the challenges. So instead of hitting the books, I played Badminton. The result was disaster. The Champion, after a year and a half, had such poor grades that he dropped out, quit — resolving never to go back.

I prayed hard and wept bitter tears, knowing the Lord's call, but feeling too stupid to make the grade.

It took two years for the Lord to turn me around. My Pastor never gave up on me, the Lord brought Wilma into my life and the Holy Spirit dealt with me until I said, "Yes!" I told Wilma, "I have to go back to Bethel."

I went back on probation for the first quarter – my grades came up – I got my first "A" and I was free from the crevasse of despair.

Eventually I graduated, now 60 years later I praise the Lord for the valley and for His steadfast love to guide me back up the mountain. The Lord is Faithful!

Isaiah 43:1 Do not fear, for I have redeemed you; I have called you by name; you are Mine! [2] ***When you pass through the waters, I will***

be with you; And through the rivers, they will not overflow you. When you walk through the fire, you will not be scorched, Nor will the flame burn you. [3] *For I am the Lord your God, The Holy One of Israel, your Savior.*

The 1936 Nash 400 (A little snow, dressed
for a date and no place to go)

42. A '36 NASH

I was discharged from the Army at Camp Beal, Marysville, CA. around the end of October in 1946. I took a bus from Sacramento to Minneapolis. No one knew I was coming home, and not wanting to bother my relatives, I decided to walk from the Jefferson bus depot to my Uncle's place 2437 13th Ave in South Minneapolis. I was tired of walking so when I saw the used car lot I paid $350 cash for a 1936 Nash 500 (500 and later 400 indicated how far they could go on a tank of gas). My first discovery was a broken frame, so I stopped at a welding shop for repair. The second discovery was a flat crankshaft. I learned a lot about cars from the old Nash. I pulled the oil-pan to replace bearing inserts so many times (I could do it in 15 minutes) that I had to drill and re-tap the bolt holes. 2 ½ years later I sent the shaft to Chicago and had it reworked and turned to standard.

The winter of '46 my brother and I logged an acreage about a mile beyond a maintained road. We broke trail by driving in and out once with a horse drawn wagon, then with the old Nash fitted with knobby tires we drove in and out all winter without a problem. One time I broke though the ice with the left rear wheel. I just tucked a tire chain down around the front of the rear wheel and was able to ease the Nash up and out of the hole to solid ice.

The Nash was the car I drove while dating Wilma. One night I dropped her off about 10:30 and headed home. Just as I turned onto the highway, the back end of the car jumped, like I had run over something in the road. I discovered my gas tank lying in the driveway. I pulled the tank aside, backed the car off the road and walked to the house. Wilma came to the door and directed me to a cot upstairs. The cot had two wings which if you rolled over on either one it flipped you on the floor. I had three lessons that night. The next day I put the tank in the trunk and ran the gas line through the floor. I rather enjoyed saying, "Fill'er up," and the attendant asking, "Where's the tank?"

Minnesota winters can be brutal. One night after taking Wilma home I was about four miles from town driving carefully on the icy road, trying to use the least slippery part of the road, when the car broke through the snow ledge I was driving on and I found myself in the ditch. The only option I had was to walk. I had dress shoes on so it was three steps forward and slide back two, but I made it! The next day I borrowed the old Lincoln wrecker from my boss, and my Uncle Goodwin, went with me to get the Nash. We pulled it out of the ditch and I headed down the road. It's good I looked back because the car was on fire. Well we got the fire out only to discover both front wheels pointing in. Back in the shop I straightened the tie rod, grabbed a bunch of wires from the trash, rewired the distributer, and headed to Church. A few days later I jumped in the car, hit the gas and went right into the neighbor's yard. The tie rod was broken.

I took a lot of ribbing about that old car, the old clunker they called it. My Mom called it apiece of junk. I drove it for over three years and learned a lot about life from that '36 Nash-can. Wilma and I have a lot of mostly good memories, but I confess, I never bought another Nash, though my brother bought a 400. The '36 Nash helped me learn the used car salesman's proverb.

Proverbs 20:14 "Bad, Bad", says the buyer, but when he goes away, then he boasts.

Roger and his first accordion, note the
bandaged finger – I wasn't playing

43. ALL TOGETHER NOW!

The winter of 1946-47 my brother Ken and I harvested trees - tops and branches for wood, and trunks for logs. That spring our efforts yielded over 20,000 board feet of lumber and 100 cords of wood. The wood sold at auction when Dad sold the farm, for a dollar a cord.

Sawing wood was always a shared-labor affair among neighbors. The neighbors brought the logs from our pile to the table where Dad pushed them through the saw and I caught the chunk that was sawed off and threw it into a growing pile behind me.

One log was an oak piece short enough for only two chunks and so large that we had to saw into it several times to sever the two chunks. The chunk I caught was so heavy I just pivoted and sat it on the ground beside me. When I straightened up I put my finger on the edge of the chunk to catch my balance just as Dad pushed the other chunk off the bench and the two came together with my finger in between.

I signaled Dad and he nodded, having seen what happened, and I headed for the house. When I entered the door my mother asked, "What happened?" I held up my finger and she said, "You look a little green," then turned and went for the first aid kit.

Mom took a picture of me that evening with my accordion strapped over my shoulders. One doesn't have to look too close to see above the keyboard a protruding finger with a large bandage.

I tell this story about the all togetherness of one's body, smash your finger and you get sick all over, to illustrate:

Romans 12:5&15 We, who are many, are one body in Christ, and individually members one of another. Rejoice with those who rejoice, and weep with those who weep.

44. SANFORIZED

Bethel College (1947 my freshman year) changed from a Junior College to a four year program. That fall my folks sold the farm north of Mora, Minnesota, and moved south to Claremont, Minnesota. In late October they (Mom, Dad, Great Grandmother, and Sister Verly) were on their way back to Mora to finish up some details and called from Uncle Paul's in Minneapolis, inviting me to go along.

I caught a streetcar, St. Paul to Minneapolis (the last one that day because of accumulating snow) and we headed north. The blizzard increased and at Cambridge we ran into a wall of snow! The '41 Chrysler pulling a 2 wheeled trailer swerved and went cross over the road. I shoveled and pushed for nearly 5 miles, until I was too exhausted to get out of the car, so we left the trailer in Grande. Five other cars joined us and a snowplow led the way. Just south of Stanchfield the snow plow hit a drift and slid sideways leaving a corner in an otherwise straight road. Dad didn't see the jog and high-centered the car, so we were parceled out to other cars in the caravan (the plow quit at Stanchfield).

We arrived in Mora nine hours after leaving Minneapolis (a 1½ hour trip). We were told that no vehicles had traveled that road since early morning.

I had not dressed for the weather: a thin overcoat, no cap, no gloves, no winter underwear, and unsanforized trousers. When I stepped into the light at Uncle Goodwin's, my Aunt Ruby went bonkers. My pants were tight to my legs with 8 inches of bare leg and the cuff around my knees, in a blizzard?

Matthew 9:1 No one puts a patch of unshrunk cloth on an old garment.

Jesus wasn't talking about cloth but about the sanforizing work of the Holy Spirit who equips us with the clothing of righteousness that perseveres regardless of the circumstances.

Great Grandpa George and Great Grandma Maria Nichols

45. IT'S OKAY!

All my Grandparents lived in Mora, Minnesota. When the folks took a little trip and didn't want tag longs, or knew we would be bored, or perhaps because we didn't want to go along, my brother and sisters often stayed at Grandpa and Grandma's.

Dad and Mom sold the farm in 1947 and moved as far south of Minneapolis as they had been north, so in 1948 I got a job in Mora and stayed with Grandpa and Grandma (Joe and Gladys) Gruver. They had built a room on the side of their house so they could care for my Great Grandma, Maria (Kibbie) Nichols (age 88).

One day Gladys and Maria were sitting at the breakfast table sharing some exciting news they had received in the mail. A recently married friend of the family had delivered a baby and wanted everyone to know about the wonderful gift they had received.

Great Grandma went into her room, pulled out a calendar and counted the months since the wedding, and returning to the table announced, "It's okay."

I couldn't believe what I heard. Why, I wondered, do we keep track of dates like that? Why are we so eager to approve or disapprove another's behavior? Then I put my foot in my mouth and said, "It sounds like a guilty conscience to me."

It seems we are often much to eager to quote verses like Matthew 7:1, "Judge not," and then do what Great Grandma did, judge. The passage doesn't say don't judge but in its entirety it really says:

Matthew 7:1-2 Do not judge so that you will not be judged. [2] For in the way you judge, you will be judged; and by your standard of measure, it will be measured to you.

Grandma Burke as I remembered her – she was a real prayer warrior

46. GOING HOME

*E*llen *Katrine Adamson, born November 30, 1875, married George Burke March 21, 1899. The only remaining records after the Court House at Watson, MN burned, listed their first born as a boy baby. The actual name of that boy was Verdy Willie, born Feb. 1, 1900, and he was my father.*

Grandma, as a young girl, had a vision in which Jesus told her she would live to see Him come in the clouds and she would be caught up to meet him in the air.

As she grew older her health began to fail. Doctors at the University Hospital in Minneapolis, MN performed several severe surgeries and sent her home with limited prospects of living more than a few months. Grandma was a tough gal and fooled them, living six or seven years before her health failed.

Her family doctor (Dr. Bossert) contacted the University Hospital for information regarding her treatment. The return info said, "This can not be the same Ellen Burke we treated. It would be impossible, after the extensive surgery she received, to still be alive." But she was!

Grandma drifted in and out of consciousness before slipping into a deep coma. Then suddenly she roused herself and said, "Jesus came to take me home, but I told Him He had promised I would live until He came in the clouds and he left." Grandpa, a crusty old guy, couldn't handle it any more, he said, "Ma, if Jesus comes again, you tell Him you're ready."

She closed her eyes and a short time later slipped into the presence of her Lord, January 2, 1950. She didn't know the how or when, but she knew Him! And now she is where she belongs, home with Him forever.

2 Corinthians 5:6 Therefore, being always of good courage, and knowing that while we are at home in the body we are absent from the Lord.

47. THE JOURNEY

Dan to Beersheba refers not just to a long trip but the total involvement of everything in between the two extremities. If Dan represents my physical birth and Beersheba my death, then everything in between describes my response to the opportunities in between. Physically I was born August 1, 1926 and somewhere around age 9 at VBS I was born again. The problem was that nothing changed. I still controlled my destiny, or so I thought. I catered to my desires and was often unsatisfied by the results.

Then came August of 1944, just after my 18th birthday, and life made a dramatic turn; I surrendered, as best I could, to the Lordship of Jesus Christ. The following April, the 26th I was baptized and joined the Hillman Baptist Church and on May 9th at Fort Snelling, I took the oath to serve in the U.S. Army and defend my country.

I returned to the States from Japan in 1946 and the following Fall began my first year at Bethel College. During my sophomore year I heard evangelist Ernest Rockstadt, speaking at the annual "Deeper Life Week" about the "Crucified Life." Those were good heartwarming messages enjoyed by many, including me.

I was a student pastor at the time (1948) serving one of the Hillman Baptist's satellite churches. Services were in a rural school called "Little Ann." The Trupe family (Wilma Trupe would become my wife) worshipped there and they were also members at Hillman.

That fall the Hillman church invited Rev. Rockstadt to preach the same series he had preached at Bethel. I attended every night and finally under the convicting power of the Holy Spirit I slipped out of my seat, made my way to the altar, and with many tears gave myself to Jesus. As I prayed I became aware that Wilma was kneeling next to me also giving herself to the Lordship of Jesus. What freedom and joy filled our hearts that night.

That was not the end, a sure ticket to heaven, but a renewed beginning for a lifetime of learning how to live Crucified and yet be vitally alive in this world for Jesus.

Romans 6:6-8 and 11 Knowing this, that our old self was crucified with Him, in order that our body of sin might be done away with, so that we would no longer be slaves to sin; [7] *for he who has died is freed from sin.* [8] *Now if we have died with Christ, we believe that we shall also live with Him.* [11] *Even so consider yourselves to be dead to sin, but alive to God in Christ Jesus.*

48. TENACITY

A college friend accepted an eight week summer assignment to join a team and go to upper Michigan to hold Bible Schools in some of our Baptist General Conference churches. He said goodbye to his wife and children and headed north. He almost finished three weeks before he was so homesick he abandoned the team and came home.

A missionary friend, Norma Harris, said that you had to be a little stubborn, even bullheaded, or you would never make it in the mission field. I think a better word is "tenacious" in the sense of hanging on, being steadfast, persevering, a prized character trait. We ought to be people who finish the course!

I think I qualify. I began Bethel College and Seminary in September of 1947 and finished seventeen years later. Perhaps I'm a slow learner, but I had a family and needed food, clothing, shelter, besides tuition, fees, books, etc.

You have no doubt heard of the "Patience of Job". His wasn't a quiet resolve, it was a tenacious battle. He wondered, as we often do, "Why is this happening to me?"

I have asked that question too, but my answer eventually became, "Why not?" The axe may be dull but eventually with enough strokes you will bring the tree down. So why not try a little harder? Keep your eye on the goal and keep on keeping on.

Jesus said, "It is finished." The Apostle Paul said, "I have finished the course." Finishing is what burned in my soul! And by the grace of God with tenacity we kept plodding towards the goal and in May 1964 we finished the course. I wore the cap and received the sheep skin!

1 Corinthians 15:58 Therefore, my beloved brethren, be steadfast, immovable, always abounding in the work of the Lord, knowing that your toil is not in vain in the Lord.

49. HUMILIATION

Humiliation is not the same as being humble no more than meekness is weakness. Someone said that "meekness is strength under control". In like manner humility is the strength of knowing who you are, or more properly, whose you are. Humiliation is the result of discovering the reality you didn't know.

It was time for our regular trip to the doctor with our first born, who was now a toddler. While we waited in the reception area, Marjorie had the usual small child's problem resulting in a dozen or so small marbles escaping her diaper and rolling around on the floor. Wilma, the typical Mom, saw what was happening and asked for my hankie. She picked up the offensive articles, wrapped them in my hankie (unbeknownst to me) and I placed the packet in my coat pocket.

A little while later I felt a sneeze coming on so I pulled my hankie out of my pocket, snapped it straight and sprayed the contents all over the room.

Wilma was humble but I was humiliated. She performed a servant role while I, without understanding proceeded to make a fool of myself.

Humility demonstrates itself by serving. Humiliation is the result of demonstrating one's ignorance.

Dishonor and humiliation, according to Psalm 44:15, overwhelms. And Proverbs 15:33 says that "humility comes before honor."

Jesus said, "The meek shall inherit the earth," while Peter and James report that God is opposed to the proud but gives grace to the humble.

James 4:10 Humble yourselves in the presence of the Lord, and He will exalt you.

50. THE BEST POLICY

I began working for the Fisher Pontiac – GMC Garage in Mora, Minnesota in 1948. It was the traditional full service operation and I was the grease monkey, car jockey, tire repairer; wash - vacuum, grease and lubrication specialist.

Wally Hoyer was the office manager and Bill Fisher the shop foreman and owner. They seemed pleased with my work and I tried to give them my best effort.

One day a customer brought his '35 or '36 Chevy to have an oil change – grease job. I did the usual service and brought the job card to the office.

When the customer returned he asked if I had greased the knee-action. I said, "Yes sir," not willing to admit I didn't know what the knee action was.

Wally said come with us, the car was still on the hoist so we went around to the front of the car and it was obvious that no wrench had touched the knee-action oil plugs.

I learned a lesson that day — never pretend you know something when you don't. I'm not sure I know why it's so hard to admit you don't know or that you're wrong, but it is! It's a lot easier in the long run, to ask, "What do you mean?"

One thing indelibly imprinted on my memory is this: A lie will always be discovered and carries heavy consequences and it hurts like crazy when you have to face the truth!

I don't recall ever having to grease another knee-action Chevy, but I never forgot that knee-actions have oil plugs. The most important lesson I learned was that honesty is the best policy.

Ephesians 4:25 Therefore, laying aside falsehood, speak truth each one of you with his neighbor, for we are members of one another

Grandpa Joe and Grandma Gladys Gruver

51. CRISIS!

I've weathered a number of crises in my life; some because of my ignorance, some from not seeing the whole picture, and a few were genuine, call 911, full blown emergencies.

The first one was a 911 crisis. We were pumping water for the cattle. I was 18 months old and I got so close to the pump jack that my rompers were wound into the gears and cut my abdomen so that Mom could see my intestines. I don't recall how the hole was closed but I carry the scar.

A second crisis occurred when my folks decided to visit relatives in Hayward, Wisconsin. At age two it could have been the southern tip of Africa. I was terrified and convinced I would never see Mom and Dad again.

I stayed with my grandparents in 1948. Grandpa Gruver was struggling with heart failure and the options for treatment were very limited.

Two daughters and Fran, a 3 year old Granddaughter, arrived from Kansas. Grandpa asked Fran to sing a song for him and though she had been singing Christmas carols in the car, now she sang "Safe in The Arms of Jesus," a kind of doxology for Grandpa.

A few hours later I found myself with six hysterical women (they denied it later) and Grandpa's body. I put the ladies in the kitchen, called the Doctor and the mortuary and later helped put Grandpa's body in the ambulance.

When Grandpa died January 9, 1949, the crisis was over, the tent was taken down, and Grandpa was with Jesus. Jesus is our refuge and help for every crisis.

2 Corinthians 5:1 For we know that if the earthly tent which is our house is torn down, we have a building from God, a house not made with hands, eternal in the heavens.

She said "YES"!
Wilma and Roger

52. EASTER

Wilma's folks lived next to the Wagner Hatchery, so each year at Easter her Mom would get some baby chicks for the Sunday School children. The problem with the chick idea was that the children often loved them to death before church was over.

Many of us grew up trying to figure out how the Easter Bunny laid those eggs in the basket, or hid them all over the back yard, and how come so many were candy and not eggs at all? Over the years I have listened to wannabe theological arguments about eggs, chicks, rabbits, and lilies. It has been an interesting experience hearing about hundreds of innovative ideas and rationalizations used by Sunday School teachers to illustrate the Easter lesson.

I'm not sure why we feel the need to use bunnies, chicks and eggs; perhaps they are more palatable than the real story of death, grave and resurrection, or maybe we think little children need cartoonlike visuals to enable them to understand truth.

Maybe the problem is that we haven't experienced the cross and the resurrection ourselves, or perhaps we just don't know how to present death, burial, and resurrection to children.

Easter is the key that admits us to the family of God. The Easter message is transformational, offering divine life, Christ-likeness, immortality! It releases the power for every thing we need to live a godly life *(II Pet.1:3)*. Easter gives us hope that we shall be caught up to be with Him, live in the Father's presence and enjoy the mansions He has prepared for all who those who love Him.

2 Corinthians 5:21 (NASB) He made Him who knew no sin to be sin on our behalf, so that we might become the righteousness of God in Him.

That's the Easter message!

53. DECISIONS

If one is deciding to get off the fence he had best investigate the ground he will walk on. Little decisions have a way of determining a very long journey. Life is a collage of small decisions.

My most important decision was in regard to my relationship with God by accepting Jesus, God's Son, as my personal Savior and Lord. That decision changed forever the direction of my life. Many of my decisions were for personal reasons; some made blindly because of pressure points, some because of personal and family needs, but accepting Christ was absolutely essential becoming foundational for everything else.

I quit my job at Grand Ave. Ford (St. Paul, MN) in 1954 because I heard myself responding with the vulgarity I heard daily in the shop and decided my spiritual health was more important than the job.

So with my family (Wilma, Marjorie, Doris and Tim) I moved to Two Harbors, Minnesota. That decision put me in carpentry with my Dad for a time, then into the Sonju Ford Body Shop with Christian partners and into a church where I gained a whole family of brothers and sisters in Christ.

The next 10 years working in that Church as Youth Pastor, Deacon, Sunday School Superintendent, Pastoral Search and on other Boards and Committees, provided some of my greatest training for ministry experiences.

I look back on nearly 60 wonderful years in Pastoral ministry resulting from those decisions. I believe the most important ingredient of those decisions, by the grace of the Lord Jesus, has been the foundation upon which I have been privileged to build.

1 Corinthians 3:11 For no man can lay a foundation other than the one which is laid, which is Jesus Christ.

54. MY CHRISTMAS PRAYER

I remember looking through the nursery window at the Owatonna Hospital September 22, 1950 trying to comprehend the miracle of birth. Our first born, a helpless, fragile, little girl, not only belonged to Wilma and me, bore our DNA, but was our responsibility. I thought, what do we know about developing the potential of a life capable of becoming a saint or a felon?

I prayed with all my heart for wisdom to build into that little life the virtues necessary to develop her into a godly woman. God answered that prayer, and subsequent prayers for four additional miracles of His mercy and grace.

So when I adjust my focus each Christmas to Bethlehem's manger, it's kind of like looking through the window at the hospital nursery. Jesus is the only one in the nursery, God's Son, for whom God takes full responsibility as he offers him to everyone looking through the window. His life is a miracle of God's grace, a gift of life for all whose hearts would open to him. Every heart that responds to him discovers in this Bethlehem baby the only name by which we find divine life.

Dear Lord, as I stand in awe at the window of Bethlehem's nursery, I confess my need of forgiveness, certainly for my selfish rebelliousness, but also for assuming that somehow I'm not as needy as most, or that I am more deserving of the mercy and grace wrapped up in your miraculous gift there in the manger. Forgive me, O Lord, for taking your marvelous display of love for granted, forgive me for thinking I'm alone at the window while ignoring the whole world standing there with me.

Lord, help me grow in the abundant dimensions of faith until I grasp the enormity of your love and Christmas becomes bonded with Calvary. I recall that when Herod's men came to kill the baby in the manger, it was empty. Those who looked at the cross in the evening found it empty. When the women came to anoint His body in the tomb it was empty.

Oh, God, I know Christmas is not just an empty manger, an empty cross, and an empty tomb, but a testimony that you are a living and abiding Lord. And Lord, I remember you said you will come in like manner as you were seen to go. But when I try to take it all in I often feel like the father of the boy with the unclean spirit, praying from the depths of his heart, "Lord, help my unbelief." O' Lord Jesus, wrap me in the arms of your love and hold me close until at last I am privileged with the redeemed of all the ages to gather in true celebration at the marriage Supper of the Lamb. Amen!

Rev. 19:9 Blessed are those who are invited to the marriage supper of the Lamb.

55. SOMETHING NEW

Solomon said there is nothing new under the sun, everything has existed for ages (Ecclesiastes 1:10). But experience tells me newness is there, all we need to do is take the time to see, feel, taste and smell — the beauty, majesty and awesomeness of creation is waiting with a newness that will evidence for us the handiwork of God.

We often loaded our car with as many Grandkids as we could as we headed for a little cabin above Fairplay, Colorado on vacation. On one of those trips Grandson Chris (5, plus or minus) was with us for the first time. As we exited Denver, climbing the slope heading south, I heard Chris say, quietly, but with profound reverence, "Oh—my—I must be in heaven." The mountain had been there all the time but Chris hadn't, and it was awesome and new.

Wilma and I served a rural mission work near Webster, Wisconsin. Just east of town we passed a little lake with clear blue water surrounded by multiple species of trees: maples, birch, oaks, etc. When the trees were in full fall color I stopped and took several pictures and showed the slides at church. The folks ooo-d and ahh-d and asked "Where did you take those beautiful pictures?" They had never seen such beauty even though they drove by it every time they went to town.

So many things could be excitingly new to us if we only took time to appreciate what is already there.

Many years ago I took time to look at an old rugged Cross. I saw myself in the rags of my sin and God's Son dying there for me! That day He became real and I became new in God's family.

2 Corinthians 5:17 If anyone is in Christ, he is a new creature; the old things passed away; behold, new things have come.

56. DECISIONS, DECISIONS

We moved from St. Paul, Minnesota 200 miles or 4 hrs (I- 35 shortens it to 177 Miles and 3 hrs) north to Two Harbors the first of May 1954, and got caught in a blizzard. We rented a four wheeled trailer to be returned to the rental agency in St. Paul. The roads were coated with a heavy layer of snow and ice when I left at 7 pm and just south of Duluth I had to put chains on the 1951 Chrysler to make Fond Du Lac hill. Thirteen hours later, tired and blurry eyed, I delivered the trailer.

We moved into a house (shack) across the road from my folks and a block south of Ken and Ethel. I began work with my Dad in carpentry and planning a 1500 chicken and egg business with my brother, Ken. Wilma and I joined the First Baptist Church of Two Harbors where my friend, Bob Daley, a recent Seminary graduate, was in his fourth year as the founding Pastor of the Church. While Wilma took care of the nursery and taught Sunday School, I was elected to be the Sunday School Superintendent and Youth Pastor (untitled, sponsor, advisor?).

I had been President of the CYF (Conference Youth Fellowship) at the Hillman Baptist Church and two Student Pastorates; one with a strong core of leaders, the other leaderless and dysfunctional. So with a little experience and little formal leadership training, I became the leader of leaders, many older than I and most with strong opinions.

My first decision was to call the teaching staff together and evaluate the material currently being used. We all agreed that we needed change. I didn't realize that the Sunday School year didn't correspond with the Church year. I didn't research the issue and no one said anything, so we ordered new material which would have to be changed again in six months—bummer!

My second decision was class placement. The adult ladies class met under the balcony, while the adult men met in the balcony. Several of the older men had trouble climbing the stairs to the balcony, so at our monthly teachers meeting, I suggested that the older adults meet under the balcony and the younger in the balcony. I was not prepared for the backlash, Emma Carlson refused to teach a mixed gender glass and Erland Cavalin said, "I will step down also," at that point I made a smart decision — table it! Six months later, most of the staff had attended a Sunday School Convention, and we were having our Teachers meeting when Erland and Emma spoke up and suggested exactly what they had shot down six months earlier. The vote to change was unanimous, and I had the good sense not to say, "That's exactly what I proposed six months ago."

My third decision was mandated by Ben and Sadie Haack who said, "If you don't replace Magda we are taking our girls to another church." Magda had attended a well known Bible College and was a qualified teacher, but she had become lazy, coming to class unprepared. The class was out of control. I pondered what to do and remembered that Magda often suggested that inasmuch as she had taught for such a long time, she should quit. I found another teacher and the very next Sunday Magda said, "I really ought to quit." I immediately, as tactfully as I could, accepted her resignation. She, however, told everyone in the church that I had fired her. Three decisions and this is what I learned.

Decision making wisdom:
1. Research
2. Patience
3. Be firm.

Joel 3:15 Multitudes, multitudes in the valley of decision!

57. CANADA HO!

I heard myself snapping a retort in the language of the shop and decided that my job was not as important as a good relationship with the Lord Jesus, so I quit Grand Avenue Ford, and moved the family to Two Harbors, Minnesota on May 1, 1954. A carpenter job with my Dad and a partnership with my brother in egg production (1500 chickens) awaited me.

When we bought the first truck load of chicken feed from the local Coop Store, Ken said, "Whoever coined the phrase, 'Chicken feed' for spare change, never bought chicken feed." Our truck was an old cab-over-engine Ford with several hundred thousand miles on it, it was well broken in, so when the First Baptist Church of Two Harbors gave Rev. Hugh Cowan a unanimous call my brother and I volunteered to move him 700 miles from somewhere in Saskatchewan, Canada to Two Harbors.

We woke up Monday, October 25th to discover the first snow of the season (5 or 6 inches). My watch said it was 5:30 A.M. as we hit the starter in the old Ford bound for a church seven miles south of Broadview, Saskatchewan, Canada. We chose a route through Duluth, then highway 2 west to 59 North through Thief River Falls to Winnipeg, Canada, then west to Broadview and seven miles south to the church.

We arrived in Winnipeg during the evening rush hour. I was driving and noticed in my rearview mirror that I had at least one bicycle rider hanging on the rack of the truck hitching a ride. I decided that safety was his problem and ignored him. Later I noticed he was gone, hopefully I didn't run over him. We knew we were expected to pay a duty of ½ cent per ton mile in to the Canadian Government so we pulled into a scale but the guys running the scale didn't want to weigh us.

Somewhere near the border between Ontario and Saskatchewan, about 10 P.M., we topped a small rise and the truck died. The wind blowing across the prairie had icicles in it. I flagged down a pickup truck and got a tow back to a wayside gas station. About midnight, with a new set of points, we were again underway. It was about four in the morning when we arrived at the church and not wanting to disturb the Pastor tried to keep from freezing in the cab of the truck. About six we saw smoke coiling up from the Parsonage chimney and while Pastor Cowan fixed breakfast we managed a few winks of sleep then it was time to load the truck. After dinner we began the long trip home. We slept a couple of hours in a Winnipeg motel before heading for the border.

Stopping for breakfast and fuel about 20 miles from the U.S. border, I asked the waiter if there was a scale in the town. He said, "You passed it 2 blocks back." My brother said, "Do you want to go back?" We decided to keep going, worrying all the way about crossing the border. How they would figure the duty? Would we have to unload weigh, reload & weigh again? We still owe 1 cent per ton mile, whatever that would have been.

After crossing the border we began to hear a knocking noise. So we stopped at the Ford garage in Thief River Falls and replaced the water pump/motor mount. On the road again we discovered it was a rod bearing not the water pump. We drove the 200+ miles from near Fosston to Two Harbors, with less than 3 hours of sleep in two days, at 15 miles per hour, a very long day! The good news is that we made it, the Cowans were delivered safely and simply replacing the bearing inserts fixed the engine.

James 4:14 You do not know what your life will be like tomorrow. You are just a vapor that appears for a little while and then vanishes away.

58. SEEING THE REALITY

The First Baptist CYF of Two Harbors, MN met in our home for a party. The games included a mock operation. A dark room was divided by a sheet with a light behind the actors to make shadows appear on the sheet to enhance the imaginations of the spectators on the other side.

The operation was performed with the shadowy display of tools (axe, saw, chisel), plus sound effects (screams, grunts, groans), and facsimiles of parts removed (fresh liver, wet towel, etc.) were passed around the room. Everyone knew it was fake, but imaginations blurred the reality, making it a lot of fun.

I don't like darkness. There were times as a teenager I had to get the cows when the woods had become quite dark. I recall seeing stumps and bushes in shapes that elevated my heart rate and hastened my steps.

I know buildings move and create sounds, creaks, and pops, yet when I have been alone at night in the church those sounds often make my hair stand on end and my blood run cold.

Our youth at Cambridge came home after a week at camp agitated by their counselor's bed time ghost stories. When I asked them to tell me one I discovered the counselor had talked about the Holy Ghost, without realizing the kids were getting a different image. Ignorance and imagination often skew the truth so that reality becomes fantasy. As children of light we are to walk in the light. Creation is God's testimony and His Son is the way and the truth — light to walk by.

James 1:17 Every good thing given and every perfect gift is from above, coming down from the Father of lights, with whom there is no variation or shifting shadow.

59. ONE FOR THE SHOW

While on visitation for the First Baptist Church of Two Harbors, Minnesota, my partner and I stopped at the home of Mr. and Mrs. H.J. We were greeted at the door by Mrs. H.J. and ushered into the living room. Mr. H. J. was sitting on the davenport with an open Bible on the coffee table in front of him. Maybe he was reading it, but because I knew a bit about his lifestyle and his lack of participation at church and in our Brotherhood meetings, I had the impression that the scene was staged for our benefit.

I say that because I have been there and done that. Perhaps it's only human to want to put on airs. It's a remnant of the flesh, the old Adamic nature that pesters us all.

We were having special services at the church and my Pastor and the Evangelist stopped at my bachelor parsonage home. I saw them coming so I prepared the scene. I placed a note pad and an open Bible on my desk.

Why did I do that? I suspect I did it for the same reason Mr. H.J. did and most professing Christians do. We call it human nature, this wanting people to think we are godly, when it's really flesh, pride – sin!

The Evangelist I had tried to impress preached that week on the crucified life. I understood that though I really wanted others to see Jesus I was standing in the way. I understood I needed to surrender to my death in Christ Jesus on Calvary and claim my position of life in Him by faith. I didn't need to show off - I needed to show up! Then the indwelling Spirit would reflect through me what others needed to see.

Galatians 2:20 ^(NASB) *I have been crucified with Christ; and it is no longer I who live, but Christ lives in me; and the life which I now live in the flesh I live by faith in the Son of God, who loved me and gave Himself up for me.*

60. WHOM DO YOU LOVE?

During my years as Youth Pastor in Two Harbors, Minnesota, I was privileged to work with some of the greatest young people in the world. I remember them with deep affection though fifty plus years have come and gone.

One of the young men, Lowell Hill, nicknamed "Punky", loved the Lord Jesus and wanted with all his heart to honor Him. This was especially true in the matter of picking the girl he would marry. The problem, however, was that there were two fine Christian girls, Sharon and Ruthee. He had dated Sharon, who lived a few miles up the north shore of Lake Superior. Ruthee, upon graduating from high school, had gotten herself a job in Minneapolis. Punky had been to the cities and had dated Ruthee a few times.

One Saturday, as I was working around my yard, Punky came and shared his concern. He told me that he had deep feelings for both of them and realized he had to make a decision, but confessed, "I don't know if I love Sharon or Ruthee."

I tried hard to keep a straight face as I said, "Punky, that decision is out of my department. I'm sorry; you have to figure this out for yourself." He said, "I have a date with Sharon tonight, maybe that will help me decide." Putting my hand on his shoulder I said, "Let's pray for wisdom for you to make the right decision."

Later that evening a car came in my driveway. It was Punky. He came in the house; tears were still running down his very red face. "Punky, what happened to you?" I asked. He composed himself and told me that he had pulled into one of the many parking areas along Lake Superior. The moon was full, casting a beautiful beam across the broad expanse of water and in a moment of romantic impulse he put his arm around Sharon and said, "I love you Ruthee."

I must confess at this point, whatever professionalism I may have had, I lost it all! When I finally composed myself, I put my arm around him and said, "Now you know!"

Punky married Ruthee, they moved to Florida where they raised a nice family and served the Lord faithfully. Punky died a few years ago, we thought much too early, but God had given him his full measure and it was time for Lowell to go on home. We miss him but his legacy gives us confidence that we shall see him again in our Father's home above.

Philippians 1:21 For to me, to live is Christ and to die is gain.

61. PRAYER POWER

Ralph Jacobson, Lowell (Punky) Hill and Rodney Anderson were, as my Dad used to say, "Like three red cows." They hung around together.

Ralph and Punky were concerned about Rodney. They felt he wasn't growing in the Lord and had too many glitches in his life that prevented him from having a good Christ honoring testimony.

One evening Ralph - the CYF president - and Punky were driving around town in Ralph's car talking about the Lord Jesus and the Youth Group, especially their concern for Rodney.

Ralph pulled to the side of the road, stopped the car, and said, "Let's pray for him." Punky agreed so they bowed their heads and prayed for God's touch on their friend Rodney's life.

Meanwhile, at the Andersons', Rodney had gone to bed and was nearly asleep when a brilliant light in the hallway shone through the bedroom door. Rodney jumped out of bed to check on the light, but when he arrived at the bedroom door, the hall was dark.

Deep in his spirit he knew this was of the Lord. He said, "I was suddenly aware of a need to confess my sins, which I did as I pled with Jesus to forgiven me and cleanse me. I remained on my knees for a long time until a sweet peace replaced my tears and my fears."

The next day Rodney told Ralph and Punky about his experience. They realized it was at the very moment they were praying for him.

It was shout'n time at First Baptist in Two Harbors, Minnesota.

James 5:16 Therefore, confess your sins to one another, and pray for one another so that you may be healed. The effective prayer of a righteous man can accomplish much

62. ANTIDOTE FOR PERPLEXITY

The First Baptist Church Parsonage in Two Harbors, Minnesota, was in the alley behind the Church; it was un-insulated and its windows were old. It was hard to heat and inconvenient to access. All suggestions to renovate, relocate, or build new, had been rejected.

We were in the process of interviewing Rev. L. Ted Johnson as a pastoral candidate when he said, "As I drove into town I sensed the Lord was not leading me here," and added, "If I did you would need to get a new parsonage, even if you had to lower your mission's budget for a while." Some of the Search Committee members became very agitated and angry by that comment, but cooler minds and hearts prevailed.

Later Rev. D.I. Duncklee accepted our invitation and became our Pastor. Now it was the church leadership that said, "We need a new parsonage," and the membership voted yes! It was also decided to renovate the existing parsonage and use it for the Sunday School Department.

A day was chosen, a visitation committee assigned, and all members and friends of the church were asked to stay home. So it was that in one Sunday afternoon more than enough funds were raised to relocate and build a new Parsonage and renovate the old building.

We were in the process of renovation - pouring cement - while two kids with runny noses watched and pestered. Their family also lived in the alley but as far as I know did not attend church anywhere.

The kids kept wiping their noses the usual way – sleeve and tongue. The men were getting nauseated and upset so they elected me to send the kids home. A voice down deep inside me prompted me to do something I didn't want to do – wipe their noses with my hankie. It was hard to use my hankie, but I did. They smiled as I told them where they could stand and watch. A few minutes later they headed happily on their way home.

I wish I could say I had led them to the Lord or they began attending our church, but I can't; perhaps they will remember the man with the wheelbarrow load of cement who wiped their noses for Jesus sake and follow Him.

Matthew 18:4-6 Whoever then humbles himself as this child, he is the greatest in the kingdom of heaven. [5] And whoever receives one such child in My name receives Me;

The antidote for perplexity? Listen, Love and obey.

63. SAVED

Wilma and the kids had gone to Silver Creek to swim. The swimming pool was located between Lake Superior and Highway 61 where the huge culvert under the highway had focused the water like a jet to carve out a bowl shaped pool. The edges were shallow but rapidly deepened toward the center. There were no safety devices or life guards; you swam at your own risk, and kids came by the dozens to do just that.

It was a great day until Wilma noticed Marjorie had disappeared. She screamed, "She's down there," pointing to the deepest part of the pool; Maynard Johnson's daughter, an excellent swimmer, dove in and retrieved Marjorie from the deeps. Marjorie was drowning, but in one simple act of heroism, she was saved. Later at Gooseberry Falls, Marjorie returned the favor by saving two young boys who were also in over their heads.

We took a bunch of our Grandkids swimming at Strunk Lake, near Cambridge, Nebraska. Some of them were good swimmers and some were aspiring to learn. I was standing on the shore watching the fun when I realized Granddaughter Heidi, a non-swimmer, who had been wading along the shore, had strayed beyond the point of return. She was quickly being propelled into deep water and couldn't stop. I didn't bother to take off my shoes or roll up my pant legs. The urgency of the situation completely over-ruled the thought of not getting wet. I ran into the lake, grabbed her by the arm and brought her back to safety. It's a good feeling to be her savior.

I attended an Evangelistic Service in the unfinished Emmanuel Baptist Church in Mora, Minnesota August 12, 1944. My Pastor was Paul Lundgren, the Pastor at Emmanuel was Warren Johnson, and the Evangelist was Rev. Bronlowee. I do not remember what was said, the songs that were sung, or the special music, all I remember is that I was drowning in deep water and I met the Savior, the Lord Jesus, himself. I didn't tell anyone. A few days later Pastor Paul asked my cousin Duane, "Have you noticed anything different about Roger?" Duane's response was, "I don't know what happened but he is different." Pastor Paul followed up on that information and April 26th the next year I was baptized and joined the Hillman Baptist Church. A few days later, May 8, 1945, at Fort Snelling, I was sworn into the U.S. Army.

We used to sing a chorus, "If you're saved and you know it say amen." There were actions added, "Clap your hands, stomp your feet, etc." which are a lot of fun but have little to do with knowing you're saved. I like these words from the Southern Gospel songs "I was there when it happened and I ought to know," and another that says, "I'm saved and I know that I am."

On my way back from Japan in October of 1946 I met George LaDouceur, a devout Catholic. He and I had gone through School together from elementary through High School. He was stationed at the Depot in Yokohama and we were able to spend several hours together. George commented, "You sure have changed since high school." Maybe the proof of being saved is not just what we feel on the inside, but what others see on the outside.

There are no people genuinely saved by Jesus, who do not know they are saved.

The best advice is let it show!

Romans 8:16 The Spirit Himself testifies with our spirit that we are children of God.

64. THE OTHER STAR

I lived in Minnesota, the land of ten thousand lakes (perhaps 40,000) above the blue waters - a blue sky polka-dotted at night with stars, for 42 years. The awesome Aurora Borealis (northern lights) spreading their display across the sky in rolling color and sound; often with light bright enough to read a newspaper by,

I spent a lot of time watching the hundreds of millions of stars, all of them in their proper place and orbit. I meditated on creation when God flung them into space and arranged their paths in the solar system.

I thought about the shepherds as they reacted to the Angelic host that brought them the news of a Savior born in a manger. I pondered the Magi's response to the new star, designed to set them on their way hundreds of miles west to Bethlehem to worship a King.

Our Christmas celebration must look quite anemic compared to the worship service in Bethlehem. Awesome hardly describes my response as I think about that night. My spine tingles with the thrill of it. It was wonderful!

Then a flood of joy surges through my spirit as I remember an even greater thrill that awaits them along with us! A trumpet sound when all believers, dead and living, shall be caught up together through the star fields to meet not the baby but the King! We shall see the Lord Jesus and be with Him forever, and ever, and ever. Oh, the glory of it! Hallelujah!

John 14:2-3 In My Father's house are many dwelling places; if it were not so, I would have told you; for I go to prepare a place for you.³ If I go and prepare a place for you, I will come again and receive you to Myself, that where I am, there you may be also.

65. SET FREE

We lived in Two Harbors, Minnesota for ten years (1954-1964). I was privileged for 8 years to be the Youth Pastor at First Baptist (junior high through senior high). Some wondered why 21 year old Eddie was still in the group.

Eddie Carlson was an environmentally challenged young man. The first time Eddie met you – and every time there after – he would tell you he was the smallest baby ever born in Lake County Minnesota (just over 1 lb), therefore, he would explain, he was not able to compete with normal folks.

One day, after I had gotten to know Eddie and was accepted by him as his special friend, I told him, "Eddie, I never want to hear you say you were the smallest baby ever born in this county and therefore you can't compete with normal kids."

Several months later Eddie came to the shop where I worked to ask me if I thought he could get his GED? I said, "Go for it!" Then one day he came with a smile on his face to show me his diploma and ask if I thought he should go to North Dakota and look for a job. My response was again, "Go for it!"

The last time I saw Eddie was when he came home on vacation. He said he had gotten married, was active in the church, and they were thinking about starting their own business. Praise the Lord!

There are a lot of Eddies who need encouragement. God never asks how smart we are, or how big we were at birth. He makes us usable as we are, where we are, if we will trust Him.

II Corinthians 12:9 He has said to me, "My grace is sufficient for you, for power is perfected in weakness."

2 Peter 1:3 His divine power has granted to us everything pertaining to life and godliness, through the true knowledge of Him who called us by His own glory and excellence.

66. MEMORABLE WEDDINGS

A successful marriage depends very little on the wedding itself. Marriage depends on the kind of relationship the couple is willing to devote themselves to maintain. It doesn't depend on the expertise of the Pastor, or the amount of money spent on clothes, flowers, music, or receptions. The kind of marriage their parents exhibited is a big plus. There's no substitute for a good example. There is no substitute for a good relationship with Jesus, either. He still supplies the wine of joy and happiness for all who invite him into their relationship. But the final determinate for success in marriage lies with the couple. Marriages will have conflicts; survival will depend on the determination of the couple to never, never give up, but to work through the problems and place their trust in the Lord Jesus.

Wilma and I were married at the Hillman Baptist church July 30, 1949. I do not remember any of Pastor Paul Lundgren's counseling. The flowers were home grown, Wilma's dress and my suit cost about $100, our attendants wore their own formals and suits, the food for the reception was furnished by church friends, the music and Pastor donated their services. I had the sum total of $80 worth of lumber and enough money to put gas in the '36 Lincoln Zephyr I borrowed from my Uncle because my old Nash was in the garage for repairs. We lived with my folks while I built a 24 foot mobile home.

A few friends plus the brothers-in-law decided to steal the bride, but ran into trouble with our attendants and didn't accomplish their mission. We look back of over 60 years of joy and happiness, praising the Lord for His loving presence and for the five terrific children He gave us.

The first wedding I officiated at was Verly (my sister) and Richard Holty in 1956. I was licensed to marry, but a real novice, and not the Pastor of the First Baptist Church. We cleared it with the Deacons, the County Clerk of Court, and the Pastor said okay. We found out a year later that he resented it and had bitterness toward me, by order of the Deacons Board He had to apologize to me.

I knew little to nothing about marital counseling, (in fact few did pre-marital counseling back then). I met with the couple; we talked mainly about the ceremony. ——. The ceremony and reception went well, but the proof in the pudding is their 54 years of marriage. You aren't around them long before you know it has been successful, and they still love each other and love the Lord Jesus.

I have officiated at 95 weddings. I wish I could report they were all successful but the last time I checked about 75% have been successful. Among these delights are our own children, and about a dozen Grandchildren to date. I would be remiss not to mention the weddings at the Stromsburg Baptist Church and at the First Baptist Church in Polk, Nebraska where I served as pastor for over thirty years. I watched their children grow, graduate from elementary and high school, and many of them from college; they were like my own children, or Grandchildren. It was a special blessing to have had the privilege to officiate at their weddings.

Hebrews 13:4-5 Let marriage be held in honor among all, and let the marriage bed be undefiled, for God will judge the sexually immoral and adulterous. Keep your life free from the love of money and be content with what you have for He has said, I will never leave you nor forsake you.

67. MAKING TRACKS

When winter set in, back in the mid '50s, Dad's carpentry and my brother's DM&IR railroad job hauling iron ore ceased. They were both in the proverbial "Rocking Chair". Not wanting to just sit around they decided to cruise the country to see if they could find a stand of timber they could harvest.

So one balmy and sunny day they left the road on skis and for three or four hours enjoyed skiing and sliding unnoticed past herds of deer, chattering squirrels, and sassy chipmunks. Finally it was time to start back. That's when they realized they were not sure which way was back. After some conversation they agreed on the direction, but after a half hour or so they discovered someone else had been skiing there too, and to their dismay, realized it was their tracks. They had gone in a circle.

They checked the moss which encircled the trees — Ken climbed a tree and Lake Superior seemed to go all the way around them. Agreeing on a direction they set off again. It was nearly dark when they reached the top of the young mountain where they could see the car far below, but the slope was much too steep. They back tracked a ways and decide to ski from tree to tree down the hill. One of their choices was rotten and they finished the trip down to the car in a hurry.

Life is kind of like that! We make pleasant tracks and find ourselves in a quandary as to how we got to where we are and how in the world we can make tracks that will get us back where we ought to be.

Discovering where we are is of first importance, secondly the willingness to admit it, and third making the right decision to get to where we ought to be.

We are all on the wrong road at the beginning and are hopelessly lost, when we admit it and call upon the Lord Jesus He knows the way through the wilderness so all we have to do is follow.

Remember this, there is no mistake, no mess, and no sin so big that God cannot forgive it, and through His Son, guide us from wherever we are to where we ought to be.

Psalm 23:3 He restores my soul; He guides me in the paths of righteousness For His name's sake.

68. THE TREES FELL

I have always loved working in the woods. We relied on wood to heat our homes back then and so spent our winters harvesting trees. Trees have a life expectancy. Which ones are ready for harvest for wood or for logs depends on the experience of the woodsman. A temperature around 10 to 15 degrees is ideal and makes the chips really fly. My Dad taught me how to notch a tree so that it fell where you wanted it to fall. He taught me how to use an axe, a bow saw (Swede saw in our vocabulary), a two man saw, (and later on the chain saw). He taught me how to load a log too big to lift, how to use a chain to secure the loaded logs for skidding behind the horses.

I learned the danger of dead trees that fall without a sound. I also developed my own Murphy's Law; "A tree standing near a fence will always fall on the fence."

While living in Clearbrook, MN Paul Nelson and I harvested pine trees, some 16 feet to the first branch and 24 inches on the stump. When they began to fall, they were coming down. Paul moved one of the logs with his Minneapolis Moline and didn't get it balanced on the bucket and when he dropped a rear wheel in a hole the tractor flopped over on its side and Paul was propelled unhurt into some weeds. The tractor was another story.

One day I fell a huge pine that propped itself up on its branches. I ascended the trunk with chainsaw in hand, measuring and marking the cuts I would make and lopping off a few branches. A big branch pinched the saw, so I worked around it as a breeze lifted the branch freeing the saw and I found myself falling backwards. I chucked the running saw and fell about four feet landing on a five inch branch across my lower back.

When I had recovered my breath I crawled out from under the tree and stood leaning on it. My partner, Paul, looked up, shut his saw off and came over to see what had happened. I rested a while before picking up my saw, but made only one cut before deciding that Paul should take me home. I thought they would kill me that evening as they rolled me around the X-ray table, but there were no broken bones.

I did however spend several painful days depending on Wilma to get me out of a chair or bed.

While living in Two Harbors we had a half circle driveway. I cleared the area in the half circle for a lawn while leaving a few trees for shade. One day a little breeze came up and one of the trees fell down. We wondered why, because the tree looked healthy. When we investigated we discovered that my son Tim and his buddy, Bruce Hanson, a neighbor from down the road (both boys about nine years of age) had been there with my Swede Saw and sawed the tree completely off. We never found out how long the tree had stood there completely severed from the stump waiting for a breeze, or how they managed to get the saw out of the cut, but there it was in the prone position across the south drive.

I took the boys behind our house a couple hundred feet (close enough for us to keep an eye on them) to an area with a lot of unnecessary trees. I said, "There are the trees, cut as many as you want." They went to work, like a couple of beavers, and felled the trees, one after the other, or more precisely one on top of the other. It was a real mess to untangle, but tree by tree I untangled them. The boys not only had a lot of fun, but they had cut enough wood to heat our home for the next winter.

Proverbs 16:3 Commit your works to the Lord And your plans will be established.

69. FIRE!

Think of elements like fire, wind, water - natural endowments of The Creator, absolutely essential to our well being and yet when these same elements get out of control their dynamic goes beyond wow to terror. I have seen tornados and typhoons, swollen rivers, broken dams and flood ravaged communities, and experienced an earthquake. I have seen fire, seen it up close and personal.

I set our house on fire at the age of four while trying to light the Coleman lantern. I lost my eyebrows and singed my hair but I remember being calm as I removed my brother from the house and ran to the barn to alert my folks.

Our neighbor boy set fire to a straw pile that had been blown against the barn in 1935. The neighbors didn't have a phone so the young man ran the ¼ mile to our house to ask us to call the fire department. I thought it was awesome to see the fire eat the straw, disappear into the barn, and then break out through the roof. I didn't think about the small calves that ran around and around inside the barn refusing to leave it, eventually burning to death. That was a wow!

Some years later (1938) another neighbor's boys, ages 5, 10, and 12, found some matches and secluded themselves in the haymow of the barn to see if, or how many, they could light. When the hay caught on fire the older boys escaped through a window, but the five year old couldn't reach the window and burned to death. The men who gathered heard him crying but unable to reach him were forced to listen to his cries as he died. That wasn't a wow, it was a day of sorrow and anguish.

While overseas, temporarily barracked with the 310 Bomb Wing in one of four buildings 60 feet wide and 300 feet long, we had a fire. My buddy and I had been at the PX playing chinese checkers. We came in late and went to bed. Around 2:30 in the morning a fire alarm was given. The farthest building in the row had a truck loaded with magnesium, and a G.I. smoking a cigarette while bedding down with a Japanese prostitute caught the magnesium on fire. The next building housed the Quartermaster with all kinds of ammunition and explosives. My buddy shook me I thought to get up for chow, so I said, "I'm going to sleep in."

Then I saw the fire coming over the roof of the next building. I jammed my boots on, threw all my stuff on my cot, and beat my buddy out of the barracks. Our barracks didn't burn but the two next to us burned completely in less than an hour. That was a wow! But it also implanted a terror in me that followed me for years so that in the deepest sleep, a moving light bulb would bring me right up out of the bed.

Our Two Harbors phone rang multiple times in 1958, alerting us to an emergency, a neighbor's house was on fire. I led the men toward the house when a propane tank valve popped with an ear piercing screech. I probably had the shortest legs but was the first one back to the road. When the fire was finally out, the man, having come home to a cold house, started to light the fire, but used gasoline instead of kerosene. The ensuing explosion blinded him. We found him in the position of prayer, just inside the door. That was not a wow, or a terror. It was a moment of solemn reflection about the value and fragility of life.

Psalm 116:15 Precious in the sight of the Lord is the death of the saints.

The Burke Family, leaving their home in Two Harbors: Roger,
Wilma, Marge, Doris, Timothy, Roxane and Philip

The old and the new Calvary Baptist Church
buildings in Cambridge, NE
The original black top school, purchased for $700, was converted
into a church and was replaced by a new building in 1969

70. THE CHURCH

Moving from the air conditioning of Lake Superior to Furnas County, Nebraska on the first of July in 1964 began the hottest summer of our lives. Driving a black 1957 Pontiac with black leather seats, five kids, two dogs, and a cat, the Burke family arrived in Cambridge to begin our first full time Pastorate. The church, known as the Black-top School, had been moved into town and placed on a basement with the woodshed lean-to on the back. A foyer had been added to the front of the building to complete the church, which seated about 100 with extra chairs. It had been dubbed "The Peculiar Little Church on The Corner". The block laying and painting were sloppy, and the furnace had been red-tagged by the gas company.

We tackled the furnace problem first mainly because of the red tag. I maintained that a church ought to be first to conform to the law. The decision was not without pain, prayer and tears — one defining conversation lasted until 2 A.M. — but finally it was decided to move the furnace to the Parsonage, which had only a floor furnace, purchase a new furnace for the church, and have both installed according to code.

By 1967 it was evident that we needed more seating and more Sunday School space. I knew I needed patience when it came time to talk about the building. We talked about adding on to the side, buying the lot next door, etc. Then we hosted a seminar and one of the presenters, Rev. Wally Peterson, from Michigan, stayed with Jim Allen, father of a large family, many members of the church, and a big key in moving forward. Rev. Peterson warned against adding on, "No matter how well you do it, you still have the old building," he said. That was the clincher, from then on we talked only about building a new church. Our funds were very limited, so how to do it was a very pressing problem.

We looked at the unimproved, tree covered, 1/4 block at the end of the main street and diagonally across the alley south east of our present location, owned by Ms. Lorintina Berg. Ms. Berg had little interest in church, or in selling her property. We prayed hard before we approached her with our plan to build and our desire for her property.

I don't know why we were surprised to discover that the Lord had gone before us when to the dismay of her financial advisor, Ms Berg gave us the property.

Wilma and I were on vacation in Denver and I decided to call some builders listed in the yellow pages; after talking to a few, I discovered one not far from where we were staying who was interested in talking to me, and also visiting with our Building Committee. They did all the engineering for the building and we purchased the arches and 3 ply roofing planks from them at wholesale. We did much of the work ourselves, which kept the cost of the 40 ft by 80 ft building, with a full basement, under $45,000.

And so it was that the Calvary Baptist Church was completed in 1969. We held the first wedding June 27, 1969 for our daughter Marjorie and Terry Paisley, attended by 350 guests. The Service of Dedication for the new Calvary Baptist Church was held September 28, 1969 with Rev. Paul Lundgren, district Exec., and Rev. Warren Magnuson, Exec. of the Baptist General Conference, offering the dedication addresses.

Nehemiah 2:18b And they said, "Let us rise up and build." So they strengthened their hands for the good work.

71. FORGIVE ME

When I accepted the call to the Calvary Baptist Church in Cambridge, Nebraska, I realized that everything I said (actions and attitudes) could be used against me. I wasn't concerned about a court of law but the court of public opinion and the assessment of a Holy God. As I prayed the Holy Spirit sharpened my awareness that unconfessed sin, selfish motives, and bad attitudes directly impact the validity of the message I had been sent to proclaim.

I desired to want nothing but to live to the praise of His glory; so began the spiritual search. Among the things the Holy Spirit brought to my mind was the way I had treated Mel Larsen, the foreman at Sonju Ford in Two Harbors, where I had worked for ten years. Mel wasn't above bending the truth, cheating a little on estimates and billings, etc., and that became my excuse for standing up for my rights. I excused my non-Christian attitudes and actions by telling myself he deserved it. He may have deserved even more than I gave him, but that was no excuse for my behavior.

I remembered one Sunday at the First Baptist Church in Two Harbors when the Holy Spirit mightily used Pastor D.I. Duncklee's message in such convicting power that folks were leaving their seats to confess sin and ask forgiveness of others where relationships needed healing. Mel didn't attend our church and I never gave him a thought but my sister Elaine went to Dorothy Lofgren to correct their relationship. Afterwards Elaine said, "I asked Dorothy for forgiveness but she didn't forgive me." I told her, "We are responsible for asking, not for the response." I still didn't connect the dots for myself.

It is humbling to ask for forgiveness but in Matthew **6:**12 Jesus told us to pray "Forgive us our debts as we have forgiven our debtors." Having a forgiving spirit is not optional. Receiving forgiveness from the Lord is tied to a willingness on our part to seek forgiveness from those we have sinned against.

Mel was 850 miles away and I had no idea how long it would be before I could speak face to face with him, I knew I had to write a letter. That was not an easy letter to write, confessing how sorry I was for my bad attitude and belligerent spirit. Writing with a broken spirit, "Mel, I hope you can find it in your heart to forgive me." I never heard from Mel, but I know he got the letter before he died and I am so glad I wrote it.

Nothing changes one's attitude and behavior like humbly confessing sin to those we sinned against and confessing it to the Lord. Who do I confess to? The circle of knowledge is the arena of confession. That's why public confession is often necessary to clear the way for the heart cleansing confession of that sin to the Lord Jesus.

I John 1:9 If we confess our sins He is faithful and just to forgive us our sins and cleanse us from all unrighteousness.

72. THE ACCIDENT

Grandpa and Grandma Trupe were on their way from Oglivie, Minnesota to our home in Cambridge, Nebraska on July 31, 1965. The plan was for us to travel with them to the old Boy Scout camp near Estes Park, Colorado, where they had made arrangements for several members on the Trupe and Johansen side to get together.

Doris, our thirteen year old daughter's best friend, Kathrine "Kitty" Jackson, a neighbor from across the street, had a horse. Doris and Kitty spent a lot of time riding through vacant lots around the edge of town. After dinner Doris pled with us for permission to go on one more ride before Grandpa and Grandma arrived. Against our better judgment we finally said, "Okay, but make it a short ride, Grandpa and Grandma will be here about 4 pm."

We were busy packing when Benny Desmond and a friend rushed past Roxane screaming that, "Doris had been hurt and will lose her leg." They were still a half a block from our house when I heard them shouting, "Come quick." Tim was the first in our family to see her. She was lying on the ground with a barb wire across her leg. He could see the exposed leg bone. When Wilma and I got to "Vinegar Knob" Doris was sitting on the ground leaning against a tree, trying to put the calf of her leg back together.

The girls had borrowed a Palomino and were riding the two horses double with friends. Benny Desmond, an inexperienced horse rider, was in the saddle with Doris riding behind him. We think the horse saw a snake in the tall grass and reared, Benny panicked and jumped off the horse leaving Doris nothing to hang on to, so she slid off the rump of the horse. The horse scooped up an old barbed wire from under the grass and Doris landed in a sitting position, her right leg on the wrong side of the wire. The wire severed the upper part of the calf muscle so that I could see the bone with a rusty wire mark on it. Her hands and wrists were all bloody as she tried to put her leg back together. Wilma took one look and turned away.

They were loading Doris into the ambulance as Philip came by on his bike. Doris held up her two bloody hands for him to see and said, "I think I can put it back together." Bob Lockenour, the ambulance driver, said it was the worst looking injury he had seen in his years of driving ambulance. I followed the ambulance to the local hospital where they did some first aid before sending her on to Kearney. Wilma went home to encourage the kids to get on their knees and pray for Doris.

Vivian Robinson, an aspiring nurse, was giving her mom, Alta, a perm but with Kitty's persuasion came the short distance across the block to help. Wilma persuaded her to go in the ambulance with Doris to Kearney and she would finish the perm. We made the necessary arrangements for Marge, Tim, Rox, and Phil to go with Grandpa and Grandma to Estes Park, and as soon as Wilma finished her hair assignment, we headed northeast 75 miles to the Good Samaritan Hospital in Kearney. It was a long silent trip as we prayed in our helplessness for the Lord's intervention to save our little girl's leg.

The surgery was finally over but Doris delayed waking up. It was necessary for Wilma to take Vivian back to Cambridge, so I waited alone as the nurses came and went monitoring Doris's condition. I could tell they were beginning to be concerned as they patted her face, trying to get a response. When she finally responded, I suddenly felt total exhaustion. I said to the Nurse, "Could I please have a cup of coffee? I'm afraid you may have to pick me up off the floor." The Doctor told me that because the wound was a gouge and not a cut, the muscles had stopped the blood flow and kept her from bleeding to death. They also told us that the blood vessels below the knee were barely long enough for them to tie onto thus saving Doris's leg from amputation.

Electric adjustable beds were brand new, but Doris's bed had popped a rivet so that a brace rod hung down, punching into the tile floor each time the bed was lowered. I said to the Nun, one of the nurses caring for Doris, "You better get that fixed or it'll ruin the floor." She came back a bit later with an older Nun. The two of them got on their knees to look under the bed when the Doctor came in. He looked at them and then at me and said, "You've got to be the fastest preacher in the country, you've only been here a couple of hours and you've already got them on their knees." If looks could kill, the older Nun's look would have rendered the Hospital one doctor short.

The next morning, Wilma returned and I was starving, so we walked a few blocks to the old Hotel on Highway 30. While talking to our waiter, I mentioned that I was the Pastor of the Calvary Baptist Church in Cambridge. He said, "You don't look like a preacher." I asked, "What does a preacher look like?" He retired to the kitchen with our order. A short time later he returned to confess, "I guess I don't know what a preacher looks like." So I said, "Listen, if you ever find out would you let me know? I'd sure like to look the part if I can."

That day was Sunday and it was necessary for me to return to Cambridge for the Worship Service. I drove back to Kearney in a heavy rain. I was North of Holdrege, about two miles south of the interstate when I heard the right rear tire blow out. I could see a filing station about a half mile ahead of me as I sat there watching the rain bounce off the hood of the car. I knew I had to change the tire. I was wearing the only suit I owned and didn't have a rain coat; so I prayed, "Lord if it would please you to stop this rain long enough for me to change the tire, I would be so grateful." I had hardly finished my prayer when the rain stopped. I hurried as I changed the tire and as I slammed the trunk lid, it began to rain heavily and rained the rest of the way to Kearney.

When we finally brought Doris home, because they had trimmed so much of the jagged edge of the muscle she was tip toeing on her right leg with the stipulation that she couldn't ride the horse until she could get her heel to the ground. The day finally came, her heel touched the ground and she rushed to see the Doctor. He, with a twinkle in his eye, granted her permission to ride the horse. I don't think she rode more than once or twice after that, but she did what she felt she had to do, ride that horse! (We just learned after 45 years that Doris cheated and rode before the Doctor okayed it.)

We didn't have health insurance, but Roy Jackson, Kitty's dad, told me that they had a $5000 liability policy. "If it doesn't cover the expense," he said, "you will have to sue me for the additional coverage to kick in." I'm glad the bill was $4099 and I didn't have to sue my neighbor.

We had been memorizing Scripture during our Sunday evening services. It was the Lord's way of preparing us. The verse we memorized prior to the accident came from Phillip's translation of I Peter.

I Peter 5:7. Throw the entire weight of your anxiety on Him for you are His personal concern.

That's what sustained us, kept me off the floor, through that long ordeal of waiting to see if our little girl would have a leg, or prosthesis.

Now 45 years later, Doris still bears the scar, and has some arthritic discomfort, but is grateful to the Lord for her leg. We will never forget the black cloud that changed our lives that day, July 31, 1965, and the grace of God that sustained us.

73. THE MIRACLE LADY

I met Virginia Gunn one Sunday evening at the Cambridge Nebraska hospital, on my way to visit a member of the church. I turned right instead of left and entered a room with two ladies I didn't know. I introduced myself and Virginia responded, "I've been praying all day that God would send someone to help me get my life straightened out with the Lord".

The Church service was about to start so I prayed, left a copy of the New Testament, and promised to come back the next day. Monday I visited her — she had been awake most of the night reading the Scripture and praying. The Holy Spirit had prepared her heart, making it easy to lead her to faith in the Lord Jesus Christ.

She didn't know X-ray would reveal that cancer had eaten part of her hip and spine. She didn't know her ovaries would be removed to stop the cancer cells from spreading. She didn't know they would send her to Hastings for radiation, but every time a new procedure was introduced we would pray and God would give her a measure of victory.

I read: *James 5:14-16 Is anyone among you sick? Then he must call for the elders of the church and they are to pray over him, anointing him with oil in the name of the Lord;* *15* *and the prayer offered in faith will restore the one who is sick, and the Lord will raise him up, and if he has committed sins, they will be forgiven him.*

I told her our Deacons were available. Acting on her request, we had a prayer and anointing service in her room, for her healing.

A month of therapy after radiation then an X-ray and Dr. Harris reported that the cancer and its damage were gone! She was whole again. Her neighbors called her the, "Miracle Lady of Arapahoe."

74. SUFFERING

It was just before Christmas and I was making rounds at the Cambridge, Nebraska hospital when Mrs. Harpts, the hospital administrator, asked me to visit a lady dying of cancer and needing a pastor. I stepped into the room, introduced myself, and met Louisa Grosch. She informed me she had not been in church for 40 years. She said, "I was hit on the head with a stove poker at a business meeting, so I never went back".

I replied, "I guess I wouldn't have gone back either, but you should have found a church where you could worship the Lord Jesus." She agreed, and to shorten a long story, she confessed her sin and opened her heart to embrace Jesus.

I visited her nearly every day while the cancer consumed more and more of her body; the stench from the cancer was horrible. The morphine had slowly failed to control her pain, while Louisa's faith grew stronger and more evident.

The last time I visited her, I could see the pain etched on her face. I said, "Louisa you're having a lot of pain today, aren't you?" I'll never forget her crystal clear blue eyes and the little smile on her face as she responded, "Pastor, when I think how much Jesus suffered for me, I don't have any pain."

I left her room that day praising the Lord for the renewal of the inner man, allowing us to triumph in our temporal affliction (II Corinthians 4).

About two hours later I received a message from the Hospital that Louisa had moved from her temporary tent to her eternal house in the heavens. What a testimony I had to share at her funeral January 2, 1966.

2 Corinthians 4:7 But we have this treasure in earthen vessels, so that the surpassing greatness of the power will be of God and not from ourselves.

75. DUBIOUS EXPEDITIONS

Why did the chicken cross the road? Answer: To get to the other side. Was reaching the other side necessary? I've often wondered why mountain climbers take such high risk climbs. How many have died on Mt. Hood, or Mt. Everest? What drives a Charles Lindburg, or an Amelia Earhart?

Do you remember "Ada the Ayrshire"? I remember a cartoon in which Ada had stretched her neck through the fence but around the post and was eating beside her front feet. This "the grass is greener on the other side of the fence" mentality seems to infect us all.

Bob Lockenour, the Funeral Director in Cambridge, called me three days before Christmas 1970 to ask, "Can you pick up a body for me in Rochester, Minnesota?" I often drove Bob's Pontiac station wagon to pick up or deliver cadavers for him. I left Cambridge about 5:30 that evening and by the time I reached Ames, Iowa I was driving on glare ice. While the big Pontiac held the road remarkably well, I watched semis, trucks, and cars slide off the road. Every truck stop was full so there was no opportunity to get off the road. I remember gripping the wheel until it was hard to let go. The question, "Was that trip worth the risk of driving 600 miles on icy roads?" The body certainly wasn't going anywhere. Would a few hours, or a days delay have created some kind of catastrophic condition?

Wilma and I, with three month old Marjorie, were heading home after Christmas with Grandpa and Grandma Trupe. The Trupes lived about as far north as we south of Minneapolis (75 miles +/-). It was snowing hard as we passed through St. Paul. We switched from Highway 52 to 56, and just east of Northfield, discovered the snow plows had given up - we were on our own. Mile after mile the light and fluffy snow drifts were often deeper than the headlights on our 1947 Dodge; we counted over twenty cars abandoned between Kenyon and West Concord, a 15 mile stretch that seemed forever. When we reached Claremont the generator wasn't charging, and the headlights were barely visible, because the fan belt was running in ice. The question: Why did we put ourselves and our baby at such risk?

I was trying to visit some folks during a snow storm in the winter of 1975, the drifts were substantial but I plowed through them and knocked on door after door and found no one at home. I felt a bit foolish for being out in such weather, but kept on with no results. On my way back to town I decided to stop at the Bit-O-Sweden for a cup of coffee. I was pleasantly surprised to discover most of the folks I had tried to call on, were also having coffee at the "Bit". Why?

Maybe it's the tyranny of the urgent, or the adrenal surge of risk taking, or perhaps the egoistic urge that says "I can do this". Whatever it is, thoughts of failure and death are obscured by the elation of the expected victory. Dangers are set aside by the overwhelming determination to succeed. There's a lot of nobility in that mind set, but unfortunately the wisdom of it is dubious.

Jesus said:

Matthew 11:19 Wisdom is justified by her deeds.

76. THE ATHIEST AND FAITH

Arriving in Cambridge in 1964 a note on my desk said, "My uncle has advanced cancer. He doesn't know the Lord and won't listen to me. He lives in Bartley, please visit him, but be prepared, he may order you off his property." I met the man in the Cambridge hospital a week before he died. We visited about farming, steam engines, threshing, horses; I would read some Scripture, have a word of prayer, and leave. During my third visit I asked him about his relationship to Jesus; instantly anger shown on his face, so I read some Scripture had a word of prayer and left. The next day as I stepped into his room, he pointed his finger at me and said, "Don't come in here. I don't want to hear your Jesus baloney." It was awfully hard on my ego to be rejected, and even harder to tell his niece that her uncle died rejecting, not just the messenger but the message.

T.P. Cullen and Charles Hamilton and their wives moved to Cambridge about 1969 from Cody, Wyoming. The Cullens were grandparents to Buren and Gail Fulton who attended the Calvary Baptist Church. Gail phoned the study, "Pastor," she said, "my Grandma fell and hurt herself last night, would you visit her?" Gail warned me that her grandpa often tried to appear ornery; Charles was an atheist, but her grandma and Charles wife, Gladys, were both raised in Christian homes though they seldom attended church.

I knocked on the door to discover the Hamiltons were visiting the Cullens. After the usual introductions, I asked, "Do you know Kid Nichols?" My uncle Jim, "The Kid" had lived in Cody for years. Charles and T.P. brightened up, "Yes, we played cards with him every week." And, Charles added, "I was his barber." So the conversation continued until T.P. said, "Well, preacher, I suppose you came to do something, so why don't you do it and then leave."

I had many interesting conversations with both couples. Gladys was Charles' second wife. He had a married son, who with his wife, were active in a Baptist Church in Arizona, and a daughter who was a devout Catholic. Charles was admitted to the hospital, January 1971, in the last stages of cancer. I stepped into his room and the professed atheist welcomed me warmly as his friend. I read the Scriptures and prayed for him often until the day of his death. I wish I could say, "Charles accepted Christ," but only the Lord knows what happened in those final hours as death claimed his body.

At the watch, the night before the funeral, I met with the family. The daughter's husband asked, "Is it okay if my wife says the Rosary?" I said, "If the family doesn't object, tell her to go ahead." The next day, February 20, 1971, after the funeral, I was told that the daughter and her step mother hadn't spoken to each other for years, but at the watch they were reconciled. A week after the funeral I received a note from the Baptist preacher in Arizona, thanking me for ministering to the Hamiltons; Gladys also requested material to help her grow in Christ. I gave her the Billy Graham follow-up series and she finished them in a week. What a blessing to see her love for Jesus blossom. I had the privilege of baptizing Gladys Hamilton October 22, 1972, and welcome her into the church family. She had just passed her 80th birthday.

John 3:36 Whoever believes in the Son has eternal life.

77. BONDAGE

A nurse at the Cambridge Nebraska Memorial Hospital said, "I don't know what to do with Mr. McClung. He is so belligerent, refusing to cooperate with us at all. He just went to the bathroom on the floor." I told her I wouldn't promise anything but I would visit him.

Cecil McClung, 5'8" and 145 pounds, in his mid-seventies, lay on his bed in a fetal position. He had emphysema and was connected to the oxygen supply. He didn't look at me when I entered his room; so I began to talk to him, and after several minutes, he unfolded himself, sat up, and began to tell me his story.

This is his story. His mom was an alcoholic and a prostitute who had neglected and abused him and although he loved her with all his heart she failed to return his affection. When the County Social Services finally intervened and placed him in a foster home, he was sick, covered with oozing sores, his hair and eyebrows were mostly gone, and one ear hung by a sliver of skin.

His foster family's method of discipline was to remind him that he was expendable; therefore if he didn't behave they would put him back in the mess from which they had rescued him. One day Cecil had a terrible headache and his foster mother held him on her lap with a cold damp cloth on his forehead. That was the beginning of more than seventy years of headaches, setting on laps and cool compresses. When I met him he was still regularly having headaches, sitting on his wife's lap while she held a cool compress on his head.

Advancing emphysema and its resulting helplessness produced exhilarated demands until his wife could no longer fulfill his expectations. Her only recourse was to put him in the hospital. Cecil felt that once again he was being rejected and his love spurned, and retaliated with bizarre, angry behavior.

I visited Cecil many times, each time the first few minutes were for unwinding from his fetal position then we would talk. We became good friends and talked at length about many things. I told him about the unconditional love God offered Cecil. We prayed together and I felt like he gave as much of himself to the Lord Jesus as he could. I rode in the ambulance with him as he was transported to Scottsbluff, Nebraska to be near a stepsister. I remember his words, as we left Cambridge, "Naked I came here and naked I leave."

A few weeks later, mid September 1966, Cecil was released from his bondage and for the first time in his life he was free and whole.

I had the privilege of officiating at his funeral, a dreary rainy day, but as we reached the cemetery the sun broke through the overcast, a benediction, I thought for Cecil. He was free at last!

78. HOPELESSNESS

One day I discovered that Lucille McClung, Cecil's wife, had been admitted to the hospital. She was a large woman in her early 70s and extremely depressed. She had tried with all her strength and love to care for her invalid husband. His demands continued to grow while his appreciation became a litany of dissatisfaction. She had given all she could give, there just was no more energy left to meet his demands.

I'm sure they discussed, screamed, and cursed at each other and cried in frustration as his hospitalization became more and more necessary. She, of course, had to make the decision in spite of his protests and angry, mean spirited accusations like, "You don't love me after all I've done for you!" She had never been in such a deep dark chasm in her life. There was no light at the end of the tunnel for her. She felt like a traitor as she dialed for the ambulance to take Cecil to the hospital. Now, filled with guilt, exhausted and abused by her husband's continuing accusations, she was a patient in the same hospital.

So I began stopping by her room. At first we talked about her family, her parents and siblings – a non-threatening conversation, allowing her to bring up the real pressing problems with Cecil. I would read some Scripture and pray for her and her family and then leave. Dr. George Harris, her physician and a deacon in my church, told me that in a few days they would be transferring her to the Ingleside Care Facility in Hastings, Nebraska for psychiatric observation and treatment.

Knowing I had but a small window of time to help her find the peace Jesus offers all who will trust Him, I began to share with her how much Jesus loved her and Cecil. I told her Jesus could make reconciliation possible and she could have real love and peace in her heart. Her first response seemed to be quite positive, so I asked, "Lucille, would you like to ask Jesus to come into your heart. She said, "Yes, I would."

I don't know if it was the look in her eyes or the tone of her voice, but I sensed she didn't understand. I said, "Lucille, Jesus is Savior and Lord. What you are about to do is to trust Him with your life. You are turning the controls of your life over to Him." There was silence for a moment – then she turned her face away from me and said, "No body is going to tell me what to do."

The next day in the hall Dr. Harris informed me that Lucille didn't want me to visit her any more. She said I was bothering her. I responded, "Doc, that's what she told me about you. He too had been witnessing to her and she told me Dr. Harris has been talking to me about religion and I wish he would quit. She had decided to shut us both out.

The last time I saw Lucille was at Cecil's funeral. She was still suffering from depression; her face reflected the emptiness and hopelessness that gripped her soul. Though she was surrounded by family and friends, she faced the reality of her greatest enemy, death, alone.

Hebrews 9:27 (NASB) And inasmuch as it is appointed for men to die once and after this comes judgment.

79. PRAYING FOR DEATH

Lyndon Johnson's presidential Thanksgiving proclamation in 1968 was prefaced with this line: "Americans may be more inclined to ask God's mercy and guidance than for blessings". He included a reminder to pray for peace in Vietnam and for renewed determination to bridge our division (probably referring to the Hippies subculture rampant at that time).

We were enjoying our Thanksgiving meal, Marge had come home from College and our family was complete. Wilma had prepared a very tasty meal, then just as we were finishing dinner the phone rang—it was the Hospital, Nancy Barber had been severely injured in a one car accident. Her parents, Joe and Joyce, were at the hospital and were asking for me.

Joe Barber, an oil field worker, and his wife Joyce, had recently moved to Cambridge. Joyce and their daughter, Nancy, had started attending the Calvary Baptist Church where I was in my fourth year as Pastor. Joyce had been a devout Catholic until her marriage ended in divorce, and when she married Joseph H. Barber she was dismissed from the church and with daughter Nancy started attending a Nazarene Church near their residence in Kansas. Joe was a soft spoken guy who had little time for religion but agreed with everything I said to him without any thought of change.

Arriving at the hospital I was briefed by the doctors, Nancy's boyfriend had taken the force of the steering wheel in his chest and had some cuts and bruises but was expected to make a complete recovery. Her little brother had been ejected through the windshield but except for a few scrapes would be released soon. Nancy had a tiny scratch on her left arm and a small bruise near her temple. Her prognosis was not good. The doctors, after conferring with specialists in Lincoln, told us that Nancy wouldn't make it. The bruise on her head had damaged the involuntary nerves regulating lungs and heart. She was breathing assisted by a machine next to her bed. Technically her heart should have stopped but it kept on beating. The doctors told us, "If you are praying for Nancy, it would be best to pray for her to die." The parents obviously wouldn't accept that advice.

I stayed with the Barbers for over 24 hours, many hours beside Nancy's bed; often I and the nurse caring for the breathing machine were alone. Joyce had wept to the point of exhaustion so Joe would take her to the family room. Midday, 24 hours after the accident, I heard the doctors wondering who would pull the plug and how they would handle it.

Nancy had told someone that she and her mother had accepted Jesus at the Nazarene Church in Kansas. I felt we needed to have as much assurance as possible. So I bowed my head and prayed silently with all my heart, "Dear Lord, Jesus, if Nancy doesn't know you, please overrule the Doctors diagnosis and give us one more opportunity to tell her how much You love her. If she is ready to meet you, please stop her heart, Amen." I opened my eyes and saw the blood drain from her face and hands. The nurse saw it, too, and rushed from the room, returning with a doctor. Nancy was dead November 28, 1968. I took it as the Lord's confirmation that Nancy was with Him and she was okay!

II Corinthians 5:8 (adapted) Absent from the body and present with the Lord.

80. THE HOT SEAT

"A Pastor's duty," someone said, "is to comfort the afflicted and afflict the comfortable." When the table turns, however, who comforts the Pastor? And who afflicts him when he gets too comfortable? A Pastor under fire is always a tense situation both for the Pastor and the church. How the Pastor handles himself when afflicted has serious implications regarding the future of the ministry they share.

While serving at Cambridge we were accused by a Deacon of stealing toilet paper. We were seen coming from the church with several rolls of tissue. The explanation: The bathrooms were without tissues, so we bought a pack and dropped several rolls off at the church on our way home. I assured the Board of Deacons that if we started stealing we wouldn't start with toilet paper. Case closed.

While serving at Stromsburg a lady accused us of neglecting our tithe. The Chairman of the Deacons Board, when calling me on the carpet said, "This is the hardest thing I've ever had to do in my whole life." — The previous Pastor had always deposited his check in the offering plate publicly. The accusation: She had not seen me do that. I explained to the Board of Deacons that Wilma and I did not believe it proper to make a public display of our contributions so Wilma gave our offering along with the congregation's. The Deacons Board agreed this was the proper way for us to handle our offering.

These kinds of problems may seem trivial, but when left unsolved continue to grow and aggravate, often split churches, remove Pastors, even putting them out of the ministry.

James 1:12 Blessed is a man who perseveres under trial; for once he has been approved, he will receive the crown of life which the Lord has promised to those who love Him.

81. GOD PROVIDES

Our annual salary in the '60s was about $5000, supplemented by driving for the local funeral home picking up and delivering bodies; gratuities for weddings and funerals were 5 to 10 dollar non-profit ventures. The result was that our family, five kids and Mom and Pop, learned to live quite frugally. We learned how to stretch every penny, taking care not to appear cheap, or neglect hospitality and charity.

Around 1970, I was elected by the Great Plains District to serve on the Baptist General Conference Nominations Committee. We received a small stipend from the Conference and our church, Calvary Baptist at Cambridge, Nebraska, to help cover expenses. The Annual BGC meeting was being held in the St. Paul, Minnesota auditorium the last of June and the committees were scheduled to meet a day and a half early to complete their work.

The first evening I discovered that Wilma had gone with Shirley Giddings to a Cafe for supper. Shirley and her husband, Lee, were from Two Harbors and were currently serving a church in Iowa. Lee was also serving on the Nominations Committee so he and I decided we would eat together and meet our wives later. When we finished our meal Lee picked up the check and said, "This one is on me."

The second day at noon, Wilma had gone with someone else so I ventured down the street to a café, stepped inside, and Dale Bjork, a Missionary friend sitting at a table with two Pastors, motioned for me to join them. At the conclusion of the meal, Dale reached over and picked up the check, saying, "I haven't bought you a meal for a long time so I'll take care of this one."

That evening Wilma and I chose a Chinese restaurant and had just ordered our meal when Erland Cavalin and his wife Alma from Two Harbors came in and I motioned for them to join us. We hadn't had opportunity to really visit with them since we lived in Two Harbors, six years before. Then as the waiter brought the check, Erland reached over and said, "I'll take care of that."

Some time later our Field Missionary, (District Executive) Paul Lundgren and I, were on our way back from Kansas, having completed finalizing the demise of our church in Hayes and I shared this story with him. It was nearly noon as we drove into Norton so Paul suggested we stop for dinner. I said, "Let's go on to Arapahoe. I would really like to see how Virginia Gunn is doing." Virginia was an advanced cancer survivor, for whom we had prayed and had witnessed the miracle of divine healing. She and her husband owned the Derby Cafe. We were seated in the Café and Virginia was our waitress. She took our order to the kitchen and returned with coffee. Leaning over me she whispered, "You wouldn't feel bad if I didn't charge you for this meal, would you?"

When she went back to the kitchen Paul got the giggles, and said, "You've got to write a book and let the rest of us in on your secret."

I have learned that the Lord knows what I have need of and provides from His bountiful resources, even before I ask,.

John 6:9 There is a lad here who has five barley loaves and two fish, but what are these for so many people?

But if I begin to think I deserve the fish and come with out stretched hands, presuming upon His generosity, I will probably be disappointed. I follow Him because He is the Lord and worthy of praise and adoration, not because somehow I can get a free lunch.

82. REVIVAL

I do not remember the first time my parents took me to church but they told me I was not quite one week old. My memories of church came much later, some skewed by a child's perception. For example, years later I visited the site of the old Knife Lake Baptist Church and discovered it much smaller than I remembered. I also discovered that the ice cream freezer was five gallon, not ten as I remembered.

During those growing up years there were many traveling preachers and evangelists looking for work; some of them excellent musicians and communicators, others not worth their salt. I remember one who was pastor of our church for a short time. They called him King Fish, after King Fish on the Amos and Andy radio program, because he was cheap, lazy and always tried to get the long end of the deal. We had a reception for King Fish and someone saw him putting cake in his suit coat, so they passed the cake, and during game time, pressed hard against him until the cake was oozing through the fabric.

I remember large tents with colorful signs that read, "Protracted Revival Services", or "Evangelistic Services". Prophecy was a familiar theme that drew large crowds. I remember how Pat Malone with his colorful charts used to pack the Mora High School Auditorium with his dispensational (Schofield) view of prophecy. We also had regular evangelism crusades at church, every night for two weeks, sometimes extended to three and even four, if the crowds held up. The evangelism and revival services had the same purpose, namely reaching the lost with the Gospel. There are denominations today that still advertise revival services, even though they're really evangelistic, designed to reach new folks for Christ, while revival, by definition, is supposed to be for the renewal of the church crowd.

My own pilgrimage included Sunday School, Worship, Evening Service, Prayer Meetings and personal time with the Bible and in prayer. I also attended special meetings, Missionary Conferences, Youth for Christ, etc., as they were available. I wanted to become all the Lord had in mind for me to become.

I had for many years longed to be in a genuine, Holy Spirit led revival. Then one day I was reading about revivals, in a book written by J. Edwin Orr, when suddenly I discovered I was reading about a revival at Bethel College in St. Paul, Minnesota. I checked the dates and discovered I was a student at Bethel at that time. I thought we were just doing what God wanted us to do; active in serious Bible reading, meditation, memorization, and prayer. Every prayer room was occupied twenty four hours a day, seven days a week. There were early and later prayer meetings in every dorm and many other places on campus. My perspective has changed; now I know that revived people simply do what Christians ought to do.

So I have experienced revival but more than that I have experienced the first installment of resurrection; whereas I had been dead, I was reborn by the Holy Spirit's activity, and made fully alive. I have been given the assurance that one day I shall be clothed with a new body, like my Savior's, and I will be with Him forever.

Romans 8:11 (NASB) But if the Spirit of Him who raised Jesus from the dead dwells in you, He who raised Christ Jesus from the dead will also give life to your mortal bodies through His Spirit who dwells in you.

83. AMAZING WATER

We've all heard the saying, "water, water everywhere and not a drop to drink". Or the country western, sung by the Son of the Pioneers in 1947, where the cowboy warns his horse, not to be fooled by the mirage of water on the desert sand. "Keep a movin' Dan, don't you listen to him Dan, he's a devil not a man, and he spreads the burning sand with water, clear, cool water."

The Platte River has been dubbed the upside down river, because more water flows beneath the bottom than on top of it. The aquifer flowing beneath Nebraska contains more water than the 10,000 lakes of Minnesota, so I have been told. When I think of the millions of gallons that are pumped out of the ground to irrigate our crops, it's seems amazing to me that the ground doesn't collapse into the cavern and the vacuum created as the water is sucked out.

While working for the Highline Chicken Hatchery, the crew I was with blood tested chickens on a farm southwest of Owatonna, Minnesota with an artesian, four inch stream of ice cold water, flowing 24-7. I was hunting bobcats on the Old County Poor Farm northeast of Two Harbors, Minnesota, when I discovered, at perhaps the highest elevation on the farm, over a half mile from the nearest buildings, a three quarter inch galvanized pipe flowing full stream in January. My brother was the pastor of the Palisade Head Baptist Church. Palisade Head is 400 feet above Lake Superior, the largest body of fresh water in the world. The church drilled for water. Seven hundred feet down they hit a vein of salt water. The town of West Concord, more than two hundred miles south of Lake Superior, drilled a new well and discovered they had Lake Superior water.

Our family often vacationed in the mountains above Fairplay, Colorado, elevation 10,500 feet. We had three springs of pure water flowing near the cabin, one a hundred feet higher than the cabin. While many places in the world can't find water, how do these springs flow continuously near the top of the Rocky Mountains? Amazing water!

But the greater mystery of water is the Living Water; Jesus offered the Samaritan Woman. "If," He said, "you would ask me, I would give you Living Water." "And," he added, "when you drink it you will never thirst again but it will be in you a well of water springing up to eternal life."

Oh, she wanted that water, but Jesus said, "Go call your husband." She had to deal with her profligate life and then her misconception of worship before she could go home and convince her Samaritan friends to come to Jesus so they too could drink of this amazing water.

Why is it we have to get so thirsty before we are willing to ask Him for a drink of living water? The mystery will remain until we ask, then we will realize it wasn't a mirage, or the devil spreading the sand with water, it was and is the Amazing Grace of God offering Living Water to all who ask. And He who promised is the Son of God.

John 4:24 God is spirit, and those who worship Him must worship in spirit and truth."

The Heidtbrink family had traveled north from Gresham, Nebraska, 600 miles to visit us in Clearbrook, Minnesota. The big event that day was Tiffany falling and sustaining a nasty gash on her cheek. Our daughter Doris, Tiffy's mother, had taken her to the Doctor for repair and was now getting her ready for bed.

It is important to note here that up to this point Tiffany had mastered Da Da and Ma Ma, not a very impressive vocabulary but extremely important.

I was standing by the bed looking at Tiffany's wounded cheek when she opened her eyes and for the first time ever said, "Hi Grandpa."

Life is composed of moments, each one an opportunity to add special colorful memories that bond us to each other, in this case the simple "Hi, Grandpa" became the bud that continues to blossom for Tiffany and me. This kind of bonding is available to all whom, in childlike openness, reach out to each other and let it happen.

One time Jesus asked His Disciples point blank:
Matthew 16:15-16 "Who do you say that I am?" Simon Peter answered, "You are the Christ, the Son of the living God."

Peter thought he loved Jesus, but, a short time later, he denied even knowing Him; then just before Jesus ascended to the Father:
John 21:15 (NASB) Jesus said to Simon Peter, "Simon, son of John, do you love Me more than these?"

Jesus repeated it, each time Peter responded I'm your friend. The third time Jesus said, "Are you really my friend," Peter, grieved in his spirit, replied, "Lord you know I am your friend."

Peter never forgot that simple, honest loving, "Lord, you know I'm your friend." The bud blossomed and from that day on Peter's love never flagged even when, because of his love for Jesus, they were impaling him upside down on a cross.

85. THE PLAYERS

Our children all have strong opinions. They know what they believe and why. They also have empathy for those who struggle with the difficult issues of life, where the rubber meets the road. The point of our struggle as Christians is: how do you handle truth and love with professing Christians who seem unresponsive or adversarial?

Some time ago Marge, (our first born) called to share her concerns for a friend's church. There was a serious lack of trust in the congregation and a lot of finger pointing and suspicion, and she said, "The Pastor is right in the middle of it. Her friend said the District Rep's had tried to help but had misunderstood the underlying problems and didn't seem to know how to handle the conflict. No matter how much they talked, the problem became more embedded.

It was at that point that Marge began to talk about her struggle and dissatisfaction with her own church. It seemed to her as if no one was doing anything. She felt like nobody really cared. She felt so alone in her efforts to jump-start some kind of ministry. "Then one day", she said, "as I was praying about the lack of involvement by members of the church family, the Lord began to show me some things I had overlooked. Bit by bit the ministry of the church began to unfold. I saw those involved in the Worship Service, the Praise Team, the Bible Studies, Sunday School, Awanna Club — and the list went on." She was weeping as she told us what a powerful lesson it was for her to realize she was not alone, or even just part of a small group of workers. She saw clearly that many people were giving generously of their time, talent and treasure to provide a significant ministry in Jesus' name for their community.

How many church problems could be solved if we realized we are part of a team captained by the Lord Jesus Himself? If we could reduce our expectations regarding others and forgive as we have been forgiven – what a day of rejoicing that would be. It's time for us all to remember that the enemy is not us! The enemy is not flesh and blood! The enemy is a roaring lion seeking whom he may devour.

I remember the day I discovered that the pronoun "you" is plural in:

I Cor. 3:16 Do you not know that you are God's temple and that God's Spirit dwells in you?

We are all players, (members of the body of Christ) together in this great big family of God!

It's as we love each other in Jesus that we find His joy and His peace and in working together we demonstrate to the world that we belong to Him!

I Corinthians 12:7 To each is given the manifestation of the Spirit for the common good.

86. THE QUESTION

Did you ever hear of a preacher giving a 20 question test in a morning Worship Service? Well I did it, at the Stromsburg Baptist Church in 1974. Here's the 20ᵗʰ question: "if you had just died and were standing at heaven's door and God asked you, 'Why should I let you into my heaven,' what would you say?"

There were a number who honestly didn't know. I was surprised by the number of senior members of the congregation who gave answers similar to Carl Haack's. Carl was my neighbor when we lived in Two Harbors, Minnesota. He had been hospitalized for some tests. His brother Benny, a member of our Church, asked me to go with him to talk to Carl about his soul. Carl's response to the question was, "Well I've lived a good life, helped my neighbors and given generously to my church." I asked, "Carl are you as good as God?" "No!" He answered. "None of us are." I agreed and asked, "Would you like to hear about God's provision in His Son that makes it possible for us to measure up?" His response was positive so I explained how he could know his sins forgiven and his relationship with God secure.

Carl bowed his head and with tears asked Jesus to forgive him and come into his heart. It was a glorious new birth! Carl reached over and pulled Ben down on top of him and the two brothers cried and laughed and praised God. The next day the diagnosis came, it was terminal cancer. Benny told me later that no one came into Carl's room until the day he died, that didn't hear Carl's testimony how that Jesus had saved him.

I visited all those who answered the 20ᵗʰ question in a way that demonstrated a lack of understanding that our confidence is in trusting Jesus. Among those I visited was a sweet little lady by the name of Maggie Austin. She had been a member of the church for years but for some reason lacked assurance. She wrote that she hoped she had lived good enough to please the Lord. So one day I stopped at her house. She said, "I love the Lord, but have never tried to write it down." And she continued, "I really can't give a good reason." So we explored a number of Scripture passages, most of them she could quote by heart. I told her about Carl and several others who also wrestled with what it means to have a secure faith. Then we prayed together and the peace of the Lord broke through with assurance for Maggie.

Some time later Maggie became a patient at the Covenant Home. I remember that visit as if it was yesterday. She said, "Pastor, do you remember when you visited me at my home?" "Yes, I sure do," I replied. "That was the day salvation became clear for me. I'm getting on in years and I know my days are numbered, but I'm not afraid. I know that Jesus is my Savior and Lord. I know one of these days I'm going home to be with Him." And I said, "Praise the Lord!"

When God asks us, "Why should I let you into my Heaven?" What a joy it will be to turn and point at Jesus and reply, "Your beloved Son, My Father, is my only righteousness."

I John 5:11 This is the testimony, that God gave us eternal life, and this life is in his Son.

87. EYES TO SEE

I was in Lincoln, Nebraska at the Bryan Memorial Hospital in the men's room. I said to the gentleman cleaning the room, "I'm not a plumber, but it bothers me to see nice shiny chrome fittings messed up by a pipe wrench." He replied, "I've worked here for five years and never noticed that."

I stayed in a motel in Iowa and noticed that the mirror frame in my room was rounded on one side and not the other. Evidently the person accepting the finished product for the Motel never noticed — neither did my brother-in-law.

Upon entering a newly remodeled house, my Dad, a finish carpenter, would notice the fit of mitered moldings, (door and window frames, etc.). An interior decorator would notice the décor, while others might just see a new house.

What we see is not necessarily what we get. We need to see with astute understanding. What we see is colored by experience and preference. Levels of perception are determined by our values, our skills, and our alertness.

So how do we see each other? Can we feel comfortable around a man with a distorted face, or a twisted body? How do we treat a person with a handicapped mind? When we select our friends, who do we leave out? Do we make a distinction based on appearance, behavior, need, or contribution?

Our eyes ought to be trained so see the truth allowing us to respond with loving kindness.

Ephesians 1:18 I pray that the eyes of your heart may be enlightened, so that you will know what is the hope of His calling, what are the riches of the glory of His inheritance in the saints.

I Cor. 13:12a Now we see in a mirror dimly, but then face to face.

88. FOLLOW ME!

We were on our way to Founders Week, an annual gathering of Pastors and Alumni at Bethel College and Seminary, St Paul, Minnesota. Traveling 77 toward Sioux City a car beeped as it passed us and we recognized Bill and his family, friends from Ord, Nebraska. We assumed they were also heading for Founders Week but when we turned off 77 to I-29 for a short distance, then under the viaduct to Highway 20, Bill continued on I-29 (evidently not going to St. Paul).

Our favorite place for a good leisurely meal was Bob's Truck Stop in Worthington, Minnesota. We were just leaving the Café when Bill and his family arrived. Laughingly Bill said, "We were almost to Omaha before we realized we were on the wrong road." "Bill," I replied, "if you don't know where you're going, you shouldn't lead."

An epitaph scrolled on a tombstone reminding viewers we shall all die, said, "To follow you I am not content until know which way you went." I have learned that picking leaders by ballot, a choice often overruled by the opposition, still demands personal responsibility, to determine which way we want to go.

The one we follow makes a huge difference in our journey on planet earth. And the goal we seek at the end of the road is determined by whom we follow. When Jesus says, "Follow Me," our response is our own. It is not negated by the opposition, only by our willingness to recognize His voice, and like sheep, follow Him.

Who is leading you in and out of the fold, to the green pastures and by the still waters on your trek down the pathway of life?

Matthew 16:24 Then Jesus said to His disciples, "If anyone wishes to come after Me, he must deny himself, and take up his cross and follow Me.

89. THE GAME

I watched in disbelief as the Minnesota Vikings, with a 21 point lead at the beginning of the 4th quarter, lost the football game. They fumbled, and threw bad passes, passes that were deflected and intercepted. Oh, the agony of defeat! I saw big men cry that day.

My grandson, Zek, decided to try wrestling in the third grade. Philip, his dad, couldn't get the day off so I took Him to his first meet. We sat in the bleachers waiting until it was his turn; finally he was called to meet his opponent. The signal was given — they grabbed each other — fell down with Zek on the bottom — bam, bam, bam and it was all over.

Zek came running up the steps, sat down beside me with a broad smile, and said, "Well, that didn't take long, did it?"

What was the difference? On one level win was the name of the game. On the other it was just a game. If you see yourself as a winner, losing is an unthinkable conclusion. But if you, like Zek, have nothing to prove, it's just the joy of being in the game.

But is life a game? One writer called it "a battlefield, not a recreation room". Games are played by the rules, but rules don't win. You have to be in the game where you either win or lose.

The Bible says we are all losers, no one wins! We all shall know the agony of defeat. The good news is that the real game has been played and God won the victory in His Son! Praise the Lord, in Jesus we are all winners.

2 Corinthians 2:14 Thanks be to God, who always leads us in triumph in Christ, and manifests through us the sweet aroma of the knowledge of Him in every place.

90. WORDS!

The lowest note ever sung by a human voice, according to the Guinness Book of Records, was sung by J.D.Sumner. J.D. appeared many times on the Bill Gaither Gospel hour and I often tried to sing his kind of bass and never came within an octave of those low notes. On one occasion, as an interlude in the song, "Prayer is the Key to Heaven", J.D. said, "Words are mere expression of thought, nothing more."

So what words do we choose to express our thoughts? My Grandmother Gruver often used the word mercy. "Oh mercy," was the way she said it. I'm not exactly sure what she meant, sometimes it meant, *spare me,* other times, *that's hard to believe,* often I think it was a filler that didn't mean anything. Many folks have these repetitive words that they use out of habit.

One of Wilma's shirt-tail relatives, by the name of Evie, repeated the phrase "my land" so often that folks began to call her "My Land Evie."

It would do us all a lot of good, I think, to take time to check up on our words. Do we say what we mean? Do our words express the thoughts that we want them to? When we use words like "my land", "oh mercy", "geeze", "golly", "gosh", "darn", or "god", are they accurate reflections of the product of our minds and hearts? When Jesus used a word it had a specific meaning. *Justice* meant you got what you deserved, *mercy* meant you didn't get what you deserved, and *grace* meant you got what you didn't deserve.

Ecclesiastes 5:2 Do not be hasty in word or impulsive in thought to bring up a matter in the presence of God. For God is in heaven and you are on the earth; therefore let your words be few.

91. THE LIGHTNING BUG

A little lightning bug hit my windshield the other night. I wondered why his little light shone only occasionally while he was flying free, but after he hit the windshield it remained on continuously. I must confess I don't have a clue.

Perhaps he's a bit like me. I know I should "let my little light shine". I know that whatever my light is, it's only a reflection of Jesus who is the light of the world. Yet it was when I hit the wall that I remembered "Jesus loves me this I know!"

I knew it all the time, but when helplessness overwhelmed me, His light came on and I cried out with some embarrassment, "Oh, Jesus, help me, I love you!" Many things had usurped my attention, now trouble caused me to refocus and my little light began to shine with the glory of His presence and I wanted the world to know, I am in His care.

Why did I do that? The blinking bug may be the clue. My light shone in bits and pieces because I was busy flying here and there, with an occasional glimpse of light. But when I hit the wall, my focus shifted to the only one I knew who was the light all the time. He is my refuge and help in alls kinds of trouble!

If we care to look around there are probably relatives, friends, neighbors who are splattered on the fast moving windshields of life. Maybe if we shone as we ought they will see Jesus and join us singing, "This little light of mine, I'm going to let it shine."

Matthew 5:16 Let your light shine before men in such a way that they may see your good works, and glorify your Father who is in heaven.

92. THE PEACH TREE

We have a peach tree in our back yard so loaded with peaches that the branches are in danger of breaking off. The branches didn't choose the kind or amount of fruit they would produce. It was a peach tree and peach trees produce peaches.

The only requirement the branch has is to hang on to the tree and receive the life giving ability to produce peaches.

Last year one of the branches with hundreds of beautiful peaches broke off and lay on the ground. We thought those peaches would die with the branch, but a small portion of the branch hung on to the tree.

The branch, because it didn't let go, continued to draw life from the tree and because it did, though it eventually died, it provided life for all the peaches until they were deliciously mature.

John 15:4 (NASB) *Abide in Me, and I in you. As the branch cannot bear fruit of itself unless it abides in the vine, so neither can you unless you abide in Me.*

Abiding at first glance may appear as just hanging on, but it goes way beyond that to include acceptance, durability, and conformity. The only life the branch has it receives from the vine. The only fruit the branch produces is vine fruit.

Good biblical words to meditate on include long-suffering, perseverance, endurance.

The struggle may be severe but never worth comparing with the glory revealed by the ripened fruit.

93. COME AND SEE

In September 2005, my niece Frances sent me 26 awesome views of the Space Shuttle and space. My old Computer tested me - 40 minutes to download - need I say I appreciate DSL? Now I can download my E-Mail, pictures and all, with ease; except my expectancy has shortened to four minutes or less. My patience is still being tested.

When I download something that's awesome or special I call, "Wilma, come and see!" The Rodney Hanquist's had someone carve a big bear statue for their front yard. On our way to church, I saw it and said, "Wilma, did you see the bear?" She said she didn't because she was looking the other way.

I don't think my desire to share what I've seen with Wilma is because she's my wife or because I am such a noble, caring, sharing person. No – I think it's because I'm human. We humans have curiosity to download and because we are communal we have this built-in need to share our experience – to unload.

While attending Bethel College 1947-48 several of us gathered before breakfast to pray and share. We shared Scriptures, personal observations, and perceived needs, setting the tone and content for praying.

The lyrics of an old song come to mind, "You tell me your dream and I'll tell you mine." Because many are looking the other way, we who see need to perk up their attention by saying, "Behold, look, come". So don't clam up, speak up, "Come and see what I see."

Matthew 10:32 Therefore everyone who confesses Me before men, I will also confess him before My Father who is in heaven.

"We have found Lucius Kibbie's grave," so said the E-mail messages from a dozen relatives. I received about 40 messages in less than a week from cousins, second cousins and distant relatives who had suddenly developed a passion, or an obsession to investigate our family tree.

Most of the E-mail information would fit in the trivia classification, with one exception. The message said that my Great Grandpa, George Nichols, accepted Jesus Christ as his Lord and Savior on his death bed. I had never heard that before, the message flooded my heart with joy.

I love family, don't you? Now I am, as Bill and Gloria Gaither wrote, "Getting used to the family of God". That family prayed for me, loved me, counseled me, and one day I became a member of it as had Grandpa Nichols. Since I joined God's family I can't even express the delight in my soul for the wonderful brothers and sisters God has brought into my life.

I am looking forward with eagerness for a great family reunion, (Gaither's again) "when all God's children get home". And quoting another great hymn, "When we all get to heaven, what a day of rejoicing that will be!" There's going to be a "Shout'n time in heaven!"

The Bible speaks of a great banquet when all the saints of all the ages will be gathered. Folks I have known will be missing yet every place will be occupied because Jesus has prepared a place for all who have received Him.

Don't wait until the last minute, like Grandpa George, enjoy the family and be ready for the upward call in Christ Jesus.

Revelation 19:9 He said, "Write, 'Blessed are those who are invited to the marriage supper of the Lamb.'"

95. LOOK AROUND

Some folks go shopping just to look around and end up buying what they really didn't need. Someone said, "Don't look back, something may be gaining on you". The Sunday School teacher said, "Lot's wife looked back and turned into a pillar of salt." Four year old Jim responded, "Last week My Mom looked back and turned into a post".

I think we ought to look back and look around. Spending a huge amount of time on genealogies is probably not productive, but to look again at our successes and failures is wise. We are, after all, a composite of our past, so noting the positives and negatives help us make good decisions as we move forward. It has been tremendously helpful for me to look back and discover the Lord's involvement in my life.

Looking back at my pilgrimage I discover many: young and old, relatives and friends, Pastor's and laymen, teachers and fellow students, who helped, encouraged, confronted, and challenged me. Some were highly significant while most contributed small bits and pieces, all of it, of course, filtered through my perception and response. Looking back reminds me how indebted I am too many wonderful people.

Once I admitted my debt to those in my past, the next step was not just logical, it was mandatory. I had to look around, so I began to observe and appraise, with new eyes, the contribution made by those who share my space in the universe. I heard an evangelist say, "Thank God for those two legged, cantankerous irritations that were designed to make you more like Jesus." My first step, therefore, was to realize that, "But for the grace of God, there go I." If I am a product of God's grace and that grace (gift) is His Son, given because He loved the whole world, then it follows that His grace is available to every other living person sharing space with me in His world. As I pursued my line of thinking I began to se that it's all about relationships, living in a shared space as objects of His grace. And by God's grace (gift) in Jesus it is possible for us to love God with everything we've got, and love our neighbors as ourselves.

The more I thought about the folks who time-share space with me, the more I began to realize how really blessed I am. God, in His Son, has wrapped us up together, some love Jesus and some don't, some care about others and some don't, but the marvel of it is that it all works together to accomplish a good and enduring work according to His purpose.

Maybe we don't feel like we have much to offer, but my dear friend, when you add it all together you discover one of the great miracles of God's grace, "Little is much, when God is in it."

I Thessalonians 2:19-20 What is our hope or joy or crown of boasting before our Lord Jesus at his coming? Is it not you? You are our glory and joy.

96. AWESOME SOUND

If a tree falls in the forest and no one is near it, does it make a noise? Noise is defined as a loud unpleasant sound which therefore needs an ear to interpret it as an unpleasant noise. I bought a book several years ago with the title, "The Awesome Power of the Listening Ear". The ear receives sound, but it doesn't always hear accurately, the awesome power comes from hearing the reality of the sound. Scripture reminds us, in the Lord's message through John to the church, "Let him who has ears to hear, hear". I began to think about hearing, about how accurately have I heard the sounds, and what difference did they make?

I remember in elementary school days, I would run the 1 ¼ mile home from school to listen to Renfru of the Royal Mounted, Hi Ho Silver, or Jack Armstrong the All American Boy. Those sounds were important at the time. I remember after Pearl Harbor, President Roosevelt said, "A day that shall live in infamy." I remember Winston Churchill saying, "Never, never, never, give up." I have often quoted Evert Dirksen, "A million here and a million there and pretty soon you're talking about real money." (He claims he never said it.) Among my memories are words my Mom and Dad said, which I am sure, if they heard me quoting them they would be amazed to learn that I was actually listening.

Some things I remember, are catchy phrases like Daniel Boone's comment when asked if he had ever been lost, replied, "No, but once I was bewildered for 3 days." I've heard (read) and enjoyed many good speakers (books) in my life that were quickly forgotten, while others remain indelibly imprinted on my mind and implanted in my heart. The difference is more than what was said; it includes the personality of the person who said it, what and how they said it, plus how I perceived it along with the value I placed on what I heard. All of these energize my memory process.

It's amazing to me how easy it is to remember certain comments folks have made while shaking hands after church. One fellow said, "That was a good sermon, I wish I could have heard you in your prime." Another, "I don't know if you're such a good preacher or I've got insomnia." I can't count the times folks have said, "Pastor, do you remember when you said…?" And I can't! It's a joy, however, to know I said something worth remembering. I resolve to remember that words do make a difference. Words have an after-life, a way of living and impacting lives for years and years after they were spoken.

I have often wondered if John the Baptist had any idea how awesome and powerful the words he spoke, "Behold the Lamb of God who takes away the sin of the world," were. Yet those simple, awesome words, have lingered in the hearts and minds of millions upon millions of folks who not only heard them with the ear, saw them with the eye, but were transformed by the one whom he introduced. My confidence, because I too have heard and seen and tasted, is this, "I shall behold Him!"

Romans 10:17 Faith comes by hearing the word of Christ.

97. LEGACY

On the way to my class reunion (October 2005) we stopped in Minneapolis to visit my cousins – Duane and Audrey, Lloyd and Vivian. Duane had undergone heart surgery recently and had complications - mini-strokes in his eyes - leaving him legally blind.

We met at the Perkins Cafe for dinner and had a delightful time catching up on the news from our families. And of course rehearsing our usual litany of aches and pains and the variety of pills we consume daily.

We had finished eating but remained at the table chatting when a couple approached our table, offering a polite, "Sorry to interrupt but…" Then turning to Duane they asked, "Did you ever work for the Minneapolis Gas Company?" He said, "Yes, for 40 years." They asked, "Do you remember fixing some of our appliances?" He explained that he was blind and couldn't identify them. They responded with genuine sympathy and then with obvious admiration said, "We miss you. You were the best gas man we ever had." What an affirmation!

Among the great joys to hail our hearts is to have someone seek us out to say, "Thank you!" I was thrilled to hear their testimony and very proud of my cousin.

I often think about the legacy I want to leave. I want it to be good works plus acts of Christ-like love; actions like the Apostle Paul describes:

2 Timothy 2:15 Be diligent to present yourself approved to God as a workman who does not need to be ashamed, accurately handling the word of truth.

A good personal relationship with the Crucified, risen Christ is the only way to leave a legacy with eternal value.

Our house began in the woods near Clearbrook, MN
where it was sawed, dry piled, planed and transported
to Stromsburg, NE where it became our home.

Plan ahead, retirement will be here before you know it, free advice that came from many voices. We had always lived in church owned parsonages, raised five children, and lived as frugally as we could. The question was how do you plan ahead when there is little extra to plan with?

The first step was taken by the Stromsburg Baptist Church, funding a retirement plan for us. Later a property (1 acre with a 65' Mobile home) was presented by realtor and Deacon Maurice Newcomer. He also worked out the details of purchase. Shortly after that, a house and garage, across the street from the parsonage, were given to us. We moved the garage to our new property, tore the house down, and stored the lumber in the garage.

We had served the Stromsburg Baptist Church for over ten years when the Lord in His sovereignty moved us to the First Baptist Church of Clearbrook, Minnesota. I have always enjoyed working in the woods so I was excited when Paul Nelson, one of the Deacons, asked me if I would like to partner with him and harvest some trees. It wasn't happenstance when we were offered free of charge a large number of pine trees recently blown down on an 80 acre farm by a sheer wind (¼ mile by 40 mile strip). It wasn't chance that a lady needing money to pay her taxes offered us 25 large pine trees for a nominal fee.

Paul had a tractor and large trailer, so with chain saws in hand we went to work, a couple of miles from a saw mill owned by a congenial young man — how convenient. We stick piled our lumber to air dry. And as retirement approached we divided the lumber and I began the process of planing and transporting the finished product to Stromsburg.

I don't think it was luck that Gerald Nelson, a church member and employee of a local chip board factory, offered to buy all the needed chip board at a 75% discount, or that we were within a couple of hours of the Marvin Windows factory and outlet store at Warroad, and Menards at Grand Forks, so that we could take advantage of specials. Was it just good fortune that a Mobile home frame and running gear became available (trailer and moving van), or that our electrician friend,

Don Lovaas of Edina Electric, furnished the material and wired our new home for free, or that dozens of friends and relatives volunteered to help?

And so it came to pass that on the first day of August 1988 we began to build and moved in to the nearly finished product eight months later on Easter weekend. And Praise the Lord it's paid for! We look back on what seemed impossible, that became a reality right before our eyes. It's a marvelous testimony of the grace of our sovereign Lord.

Philippians 4:19 My God shall supply all your needs according to His riches in glory in Christ Jesus.

***We thought we had retired but the Lord added another 20+ years of ministry at First Baptist of Polk just13 miles from our new home.

99. ME, A SHEPHERD?

When it comes to handling sheep, I plead ignorance. I was born and raised on a farm, but we saw no reason to raise sheep. They spread Canadian Thistles. I took Vocational Ag and was an FFA member all four years in High School. As a freshman I was chosen to be on the Minnesota State Dairy Cattle Judging Contest, held at Barnum and Moose Lake in 1941. When we arrived back at school, John Barnes, our Vocational Ag instructor, called me to the front of the class to report the good news that I had achieved the highest score. The bad news, I was an alternate and it didn't count.

My knowledge of dairy cattle is seriously outdated. We had stalls and gutters then, now they have milking parlors. We practiced selective breeding and feeding – good producers received special consideration while the poor ones were replaced and their offspring shipped to South St. Paul. — I know feeding, breeding, medications, and sanitation standards have changed dramatically over the years and I'm left in the dust.

Cows need care! Sheep don't have a corner on that. Our dairy cows were milked at regular times, received special diets, proper exercise, clean facilities, and a nursery for the new born calves.

On the sheep side I had short term experience. I occasionally took care of my cousin's flock and also my father-in-law's flock. I was impressed by what I saw as their stupidity (the sheep that is).

The Scriptures depict the human family as lost sheep, desperately needing a shepherd, and reading on, we discover Jesus as the Good Shepherd; but it doesn't end there; the message becomes a mandate by which we are to tend His flock. And He doesn't mean sheep-sheep, but people like you and me. He is mandating a relationship of caring for brothers and sisters in Christ and for the redeemed with their neighbors. Jesus asked Peter three times, "Simon, do you love me?" Each time he followed the question with the command, "Feed my sheep."

The Lord has blessed me with a great host of sheep tenders, some were neighbors, class room teachers, Sunday school teachers, pastors, evangelists, mostly they were ordinary folks whose only credential was that they loved Jesus and they loved me.

I am 84 years of age and the end of my pilgrimage is just down the road apiece, and my deepest desire continues, that I may be a faithful under-shepherd of the Lord Jesus. I can't go back and undo or redo the past, but I can press on in anticipation of the day when I shall stand in His presence. And on that day I long to hear Him say, "Roger you have faithfully tended my sheep, enter into the joy of your Lord."

Psalm 100:3 (NASB) *Know that the Lord Himself is God; It is He who has made us, and not we ourselves; we are His people and the sheep of His pasture.*

Taken in 2009 after Roger's final sermon before retirement
at the age of 83– Back row: Tim, Doris, Marge,
Roxane and Phil. Front Row: Wilma and Roger

IN CONCLUSION

We've all heard a question like, "Have you lived all your life in Nebraska?" and the spirited repartee, "Not yet!" So, though I come to the conclusion of the book, for Wilma and I the conclusion is not yet. We do wonder though, how did we get so close to the conclusion so soon?

We have been blessed with five children, Marjorie, Doris, Timothy, Roxane and Philip, all happily married; each of them added five, except Doris who stopped with 4, for a total of 24 Grand Children. They (the Grands) in turn have, at last count, given us 32 great-grands. We started remembering birthdays, now we struggle to remember names.

I remember my Grandmother Gruver at her 100th birthday party, looking at me and saying, "Now let me see, you're Geneva's boy aren't you?" I'm not a hundred yet, but I'm rapidly approaching the use of that technique.

Growing old (I'm 84 and Wilma is 79) isn't so bad if you remember the lessons learned during difficulties and add them as positives when you count your blessings. We praise the Lord as we look back in amazement at the goodness, the generosity of God and His people. We have seen the improbable become reality. We have seen the cup of water become a river of living water.

Life is a gift of the Lord, but who can measure the flavor of those who carry your DNA? The following are some bits and pieces of that flavor: Amanda, pointing at my accordion, "Is Jesus loves me in there?" Ryon was told to get his toy boat out of the bath tub responded, "I can't my compeller is broke." Angel and I played Hide & Seek, no matter where she hid, when I asked, "Where are you?" she always responded, "I'm in here." Three year old Abbie stepped in front of a lady pushing her baby in a stroller. The lady frowned until Abbie looked up and said, "Ma'am, you have a beautiful baby." Charity was asked for her favorite song said "The cat will wake him up" (The cattle are lowing the poor baby wakes.) Chris responded,"Stick-em in the eyes" (be careful little eyes what you see). Doris asked her Sunday School class of kindergarteners "What does tithing mean?" One little fellow volunteered, "That's what you do with your shoes." Marge said, "It seems to me that God works more with slow-cookers than with micro-wave ovens".

Conclusion, not yet but one of these days we hope to be able to report, "We have finished the course" until then there is joy in this camp to be shared; so by God's grace we shall endeavor to live, as Max Lucado said, "beyond our life".

James 1:12 "Blessed is the man who perseveres under trial; for once he has been approved, he will receive the crown of life, which the Lord has promised to those who love Him."

AUTOBIOGRAPHY OF PRAYER

By: Roger A Burke

Sometimes it seems appropriate to record the words that come at the beginning of (or during) a new day. Holy moments with God not to be grasped but shared and recounted; moments in which the Holy Spirit led me to the summit of a divine encounter.

The following prayers are gleanings from a few of those memorable moments, offered here not as models but with the desire and prayer that they will be used to stimulate you in your walk of faith with the Lord Jesus.

Perhaps you have not developed the habit of writing some of your prayers. If not, then I hope these will encourage you to do so. Your intimate impressions gained as you linger with the Master can live again. They can and will become multiplied blessings as you reread them and return to those precious holy moments again and again.

Whatever blessing you receive from these pages please remember it is all because of Calvary and unto the Lord who died there and rose from the dead and is now seated at the right hand of the Father belong all the praise and the glory.

Let me invite you now to climb the heights into the presence of His holiness for your own personal encounter.

R. A. Burke
Compiled in 1980
Revised in 2010

Thank you, Jesus, for your patient understanding care. Thank you for a faithful and loving wife who walks beside me. Thank you for parents and a brother and sisters who love you and encouraged me. I praise you for a rich heritage of godly teaching.

Thank you for children who seek to honor you with their lives. Thank you for the potential in my grandchildren and great grandchildren to live godly lives. And I thank you for the larger family of God, for their friendship, instruction and stimulation to live for Thee.

Thank you for your plan for my life and the brief glimpses from the past that confirm your leadership. Thank you for leading me by still waters and in green pastures. I look back and see how you have shown yourself and touched lives through me as only you can. I am constrained by your loving presence.

How much I need you, your constant care and your continual cleansing, your holiness, your strength and your peace. Deliver me from the bondage of the flesh.

Oh, that I might please you and work Thy works as I am given discernment by Thy Holy Sprit. I long for His wisdom so that I might know what Thy work is, where it is, when it is completed and where the next step is.

Thank you for the assurance that you are leading and that the next step shall have light for its day.

By your grace I shall know — hallelujah!

Amen.

~

Dear Savior, Just outside my window I hear one of the sparrows – you know which one — I catch but brief glimpses of it flitting between the branches of the trees as they respond to the gentle breeze of summer. Their majestic movement, together with the quickening pace of each individual leaf, reminds me of the blessed Holy Spirit who so gently moves among the members of the body. He, according to His divine will, touches this one and that one setting them in motion so that as each touches the other the movement is accelerated. I take delight for the times He has touched me — touched me so that others can see and feel and know Thy presence.

The music of your little birds in stereo seems to accompany the rhythm of the wind as it plays amongst the leaves. The backdrop of green speckled with the reds, yellows, and pinks of the rose garden hails my heart to praise you for your creation, and to honor you as God. How very much you must have loved beauty, you have created so much of it in sight and sound for all mankind to enjoy.

I am also aware of music, deep majestic strains of a symphony produced by a young man of talent and determination on the strings of the church's piano. My heart is stirred as I sense again the holiness of your presence.

I praise you with deepest gratitude for this delightful beginning to a new day. God you are great and you are good and that greatness and that goodness has been apportioned out to me again in measure as I have let you develop me to hear and see and understand. I long for greater capacity to know you. I praise you for your patience with me. I thank you for what I have experience of you just now.
Amen!

~

I served in the World War II Occupation Army in Japan and for a short time with the 3186th Signal Service Battalion. I had neglected my devotional life for a while until one evening as I entered my room the Bible on my night-stand caught my eye. I opened it at random to Psalm 19:14. Conviction flooded my soul and I fled behind the barracks to a secluded area lit by a distant street light. I knelt by a cement bench and prayed that verse.

Dear Lord Jesus may the words of my mouth and the meditations of my heart be acceptable in Thy sight, O' Lord, my strength and my redeemer.
Amen.

That was a life changing experience that has directed my path to this day. A few days later I received a letter from Grandma Burke who said she was praying at 2 A.M. for me but didn't know why. The exact time I was under Holy Spirit conviction by Psalm 19:14.

Years later, as an elderly evangelist, Rev Dodson came to the church I served in Cambridge, Nebraska. He taught us the "Victorious Christian Prayer".

Dear Lord, Think your thoughts with my mind, speak your words with my lips and live your life through my body, now and until I meet you face to face.

Amen.

Lord Jesus, for the future of Thy Church and the Gospel, I offer myself to Thee without condition or reservation.

Lord, I delight to offer myself. I am willing to let you have your way in and through me.

Amen.

~

My mother died September 21, 1978 at 8:05 AM, the result of a surgical procedure to open her carotid arteries that didn't go as the doctors expected.

On the 14th of September, prior to her surgery while I was praying for her, I experienced a quiet interlude in which words fled and the Lord assured me that mother was in His care.

I knew, for He impressed it upon me, that mother was going to die. But there was peace in my heart for I knew Jesus was in control. He was taking full charge of her body and soul. I knew He would take her through victoriously.

Lord, My heart is full of sadness this morning as I think of mother lying in the hospital bed feeling pain, facing the unknown — and yet — mysteriously, I have peace in my soul for I know you are her shepherd.

I place her in your tender care — with Thee there is no unknown. Praise be to Thee, oh Lord. Your mercies fail not and your hand is not shortened.

You are our refuge and help in all sorts of trouble. Having suffered in all points as we you are able to comfort us in our turbulent times.

I am comforted and I know mother is comforted in Thee. Hallelujah!

I will bless Thee with my mouth and praise you with my life for Thou art God and Thou art my Lord! Amen.

A blood clot formed after surgery and the attempt to remove it failed. Mother was returned to a small curtained room waiting for death. The ordeal waiting for death lasted from Monday to Thursday.

My dad, my brother and sisters and I, took turns standing by her bed, patting her hands, brushing her hair, and speaking reassuringly to her, even though she never responded.

During one of those times when I was challenged by the Holy Spirit regarding my own faith, God's Word was trustworthy for my own personal valley. Here's my prayer.

Dear Jesus, as I stand by mother's bed, knowing that she is dying, and very much aware of the many times I have comforted others as they traveled this pathway of tears. Those were easy words I read to them and easy words I prayed for them, though I meant them from my heart and yours.

Now, O God, I measure the depth and length of them for myself. I am so full of weakness to believe, but Thou art my strength. Yea, Lord Thy Word is truth! It is the counsel of God. It is the comfort and refuge for my soul. It is good. It is good for me. I do believe.

(a moment of silence as victory came)

Jesus, I sense your presence in the inner regions of my being, I am aware of your anguish and suffering as you hung there on the cross. I hear, as it were, your voice to John, "Here is my mother, take care of her." You do love mothers, so Jesus here is my mother, take care of her.

Amen.

~

Caressed by the warm rays of the morning sun and embraced by the Holy Spirit, I lift my voice to praise Thy name. How bright to my eye is the light flooding through the window and yet, greater still is the brilliance of He who is the Light, the light that shines in my heart. O Jesus I love Thee. I bless Thy name! The name before who all must bow and confess that Thou art Lord. Before Thee I gladly humble myself and declare that Thou art my Lord.

Amen.

~

I sit just now in the quietness of my study reflecting on Thy goodness, Oh Jehovah.

Just outside the window the night rain sparkles upon the leaves of the elm, while the birds chatter amongst the branches. I am so aware of you Lord Jesus. You were there when by your creative act of divine will, all this began.

And today, you by your Sovereign will hold it all together. So marvelous is your involvement in the world that even those chattering birds are fully known of you.

My heart wells up with the riches that are mine in this panoply of nature, showing your handiwork. I rejoice with praise and adoration that by your mercy and grace all that is yours is mine to enjoy. And wonder of wonders, I too am yours — yours? Yes, fully yours.

Yours, oh the majestic ring of it. It lifts me beyond these created things to enjoy your person and your presence so that I may please you. Then one day, and for that day my soul longs, I shall see you face to face. Then – then nothing will matter, not birds or branches or trees, only yourself.

Amen!

~

Thank you, Lord Jesus, for today with its possibilities. Take my stubborn will. I yield it Lord to Thee.

Forgive my busyness, things and thoughts so often interfere with the freedom of my spirit to receive the witness of Thy Spirit.

Oh God, may my priorities be controlled by Thee so that in all things I shall be to the praise of Thy glory. May those whom this life touches be drawn to Thee.

My heart yearns, oh God, for the salvation of the lost and longs to see the brethren built up in the faith.

Amen.

~

Spirit of the living God fall fresh on me, I need you! Yea, I long for you! I long for the fresh newness that proclaims in my heart that I am indwelt by Thee and therefore am Thy Son.

Release me from the discord of the market place and fill me with the sweet harmony of heaven. Take away my tendency to grasp the temporary and help me take a firm grip on those things that are eternal; things that belong to the citizens of your kingdom.

Fill me with new dimensions of your love so that my life displays the sweet spirit that proclaims that I belong to you.

Amen.

~

Thank you, Father, for the privilege and power of prayer. Thank you for the joy of knowing you up close, of knowing that you love me; knowing that you love people into your kingdom through me.

Amen.

~

Dear Lord Jesus, I pause just now to thank you for the joy of my salvation. I look up and know that you are there. I look around and see that Thou art there.

Thy touch on the heavens and on the earth fill my heart with wonder and awe. What a day to belong to you. Thank you for your excellence and perfection.

Thank you for the family God. How grateful I am for all my brothers and sisters in Christ Jesus.

Thank you for your fullness, your mercy and your grace.

Amen.

~

Oh my Father, my heart wells up with praise as I sit here embraced by the brilliance of the morning sun, reminded by your Word that you made it to light the world.

And, in an even more profound way, because of Thy great love in sending the Lord Jesus, you have shared with all mankind the light that embraces the heart, which is life for everyone who will receive it.

You are life, the light of my soul. And you are my life! Hallelujah! Amen.

~

Oh, God! How helpless I am to do anything about the deep need evidence in the hearts and lives around me. Unless you build the house I labor in vain.

I rest in your promise and power confident that your purposes shall not fail.

Amen.

~

Dear Father, I praise you this day for your constant unchanging presence.

The morning sun has not shown, heavy overcast controls it like the clouds of fear frustration, depression, and weariness oft seek to rob my soul of its delight.

Back of the clouds the sun is shining and, praise your name, regardless of the fickleness of my heart or how devastating the circumstances or how derelict my emotions, your love never fails. Your promises are sure.

Your life abides in me. You are my hope and constant delight —Hallelujah!

Bless the Lord, O my soul, and all that is in me bless His holy name.

Amen.

I will praise Thee for Thy mercy and Thy grace. Oh, that I may proclaim Thy Word before the multitudes to lead them as a great choir in melodies of living praise for Thy glory.

Your tender care and your constant love well up within me, caressing my spirit and filling me with desire to please only Thee.

Oh, that I might walk with Thee and be to the praise of Thy glory forever and ever.

Amen.

~

Thank you, my Lord Jesus, for the mystery of new life in the spring and the miracle of new life in the resurrection. Thank you for the knowledge that even the little birds I hear singing are known to Thee — and I am known, provided for, and loved, thank You Jesus — Hallelujah!

Amen.

~

Dear Lord, I lift my voice in praise and adoration as again I pause to remember that the heavens declare Thy glory and the earth shows your handiwork. I take note of the blue sky, laced with fleecy clouds, and remember it was your fingertips that formed them and set them in motion. You wrote the inscription of your greatness against the backdrop of space and illuminated it by that great light you created to rule the day.

I see the changing shades of autumn bringing a new richness and beauty across the earth. My heart leaps with joy at the splendor of your creativity and greatness and I bow in adoration and humility before Thee. Thou art God! I offer you my gratitude and praise.

And yet, as I meditate on the changing scenes about me, the skies the seasons — I observe that you remain the same, unchanged and unchanging. Your plans, your love, your character always remain the same. O God, how I love Thee!

I desire to give myself to Thee again so that my life might reflect the stability and love rightly expected of one born of the Spirit and indwelt by your holy presence. It is done! Hallelujah! In Thee, Lord Jesus, I am Thine and Thou art mine — Glory!

Amen.

~

In the quietness of this room I lift my voice to praise Thy wondrous name. The marvels of Thy creation encompass me and I am embraced by Thy Love — Hallelujah!

Amen.

Manufactured By: RR Donnelley
Momence, IL USA
December, 2010